Resurrection Psychology

Resurrection Psychology

An Understanding of Human Personality
Based on the Life and Teachings of Jesus

Margaret
G. Alter

A Campion Book

Loyola University Press
Chicago

Loyola University Press
3441 N. Ashland Ave.
Chicago, Illinois 60657

Cover and interior design by Nancy Gruenke

Library of Congress Cataloging-in-Publication Data

Alter, Margaret G., 1937-
    Resurrection psychology : an understanding of human personality
based on the life and teachings of Jesus / by Margaret G. Alter.
        p.   cm.
    Includes bibliographical references and index.
    ISBN 0-8294-0782-0
    1. Jesus Christ–Psychology. 2. Christianity–Psychology.
3. Psychology and religion. 4. Christian life. I. Title.
BT590.P9A48   1994   94-14928
201'.9–dc20   CIP

For my children:
Kim,
David,
and Lisa.

That they may spend a lifetime
discovering the depth of God's love for them.

Contents

Foreword

Books about change are dangerous, troublesome, challenging, stirring. This is one of those books.

It reflects the changing times. And it calls for further change. Taken seriously, Dr. Alter's message would deconstruct much of what is precious to the worlds she dares to enter—the worlds of self-talk, friendship, the church, the human community, and the now-intersecting worlds of psychology and theology.

First, the changing times. In her fascinating study of *The Person in Psychology*, Mary Stewart Van Leeuwen (1985) documents how therapeutic practices are being transformed. In times past, she notes, many therapists comported themselves as little more than reprojection screens.

The therapist was to maintain objectivity, a value-neutral position. She was not to shape the therapeutic enterprise by her own conceivably alien value-commitments. With postmodernism, however, more and more the folly of this stance has been recognized. Irrespective of what we might contend should or wish would happen, the anthropological fact is that none of us is capable of escaping our own stories sufficiently to occupy a privileged position of objectivity. For Van Leeuwen, then, the *person* in psychology refers not only to the fundamental nature of those with whom psychologists interact, but also, and equally, to the character and commitments of those who "do" psychology.

A parallel account could be written with regard to contemporary Jesus-studies. Already the earliest quest of the historical Jesus in the eighteenth and nineteenth centuries was governed by the task of rescuing the real Jesus, the objective Jesus, from the incriminating clutches of the institutional church. And from the late nineteenth century, scholars developed instruments by which to extract the authentic Jesus from the subjective interpretations of the earliest churches. The Gospels themselves were mired in theological interests, it was thought—interests that disallowed their capacity to reveal "Jesus as he really was." Objective scholarship could recover the authentic Jesus—or so it was claimed.

However, as in psychology, so in Jesus-studies, increasingly the myth of objectivity has been exposed.[1] With regard to the latter, we understand better today that the "hard data" about Jesus is already and irretrievably woven into a web of signification. The "facts" about Jesus are not value-neutral. Nor is the study of Jesus value-neutral, for the quality of our own questions shape already the answers for which we seek, just as our traditions and life experiences help to configure the sort of testimony to which our eyes will be sensitive.

Of course, a number of persons in the Christian world have never been happy with the objectivistic aspirations and/or presumptions of either psychotherapy or academic study of the Gospels. Christians, they maintained, are not value-neutral but heavily committed, deeply implicated in a preunderstanding of the *revealed* nature of humanity. Outside the Christian community, too, and outside therapeutic circles, the death knell of our society's commitment to value-neutrality—in education, psychotherapy, and intercultural relations—has repeatedly been sounded (see Freadman and Miller 1992, 51–71).

Whether new or old, the recognition of our existence as culture- and tradition-embodied persons, of *storied* persons, foregrounds a question as persistent as it is haunting: Well, then, *whose* values? yours? mine? theirs? Christians have wanted to reply, Those of Jesus. But how does one certify that we have not simply read our own values back onto Jesus?

This is the challenge that books like the present one must face. And, unfortunately, the track record of such books has little by way of success to record. Those of us who have been interested in the possible interface between psychology and the gospel story have been served a steady, unimaginative diet of Jesus dressed up as "my favorite personality theorist." A rose by any other name? There is the Freudian Jesus, the Jungian Jesus, the Rogerian Jesus, the Ericksonian Jesus, the Self-Help Jesus, and so on. Or, in circles less enamored with psychotherapy as a field of study but nevertheless interested in counseling, Jesus has been embraced as the model thera-pist, his words extracted from their Gospel contexts as exem-plars of "Christian counseling."

Thus, Jesus is conscripted to legitimate one's own program of therapy or theory of human development and interaction. "This is Jesus' way" is better than any Good Housekeeping seal—any certification from the state or the American Association of Pastoral Counselors. After all, it provides the *divine imprimatur.*

Dr. Alter is hardly value-neutral in her approach. But nei-ther has she simply read her case notes into the mouth of Jesus. Rather, at the same time she has been engaged in pri-vate practice as a psychotherapist, she has listened carefully to the voice of Jesus in the Gospels, followed his interactions with others in their stories, and engaged responsively the ever-growing scholarly literature on the historical Jesus. Unlike some New Testament scholars, who portray their work as "eavesdropping on an ancient conversation," Dr. Alter has been involved in an ongoing interaction with voices ancient and (post)modern. In her own practices she has realized the promise of anthropology as cultural critique (Marcus and Fischer 1986)—that this mysterious and all-too-troubling Jesus (1) can be understood in fresh ways by persons culturally removed from him and, more importantly, (2) when allowed to speak, continues to challenge cultures that are not his own.

This is precisely why Dr. Alter's message is itself so engag-ing. Of course it raises questions about the way two disci-plines like psychology and New Testament studies might interact if their guilds were to allow the barriers to drop. But it does so precisely by pointing the way forward for new ways of relating, and not only across academic disciplines.

And this has far-reaching implications for how we under-stand the relationship between psychology and the gospel story. Dr. Alter's challenge here is relentless, but it also addresses our deepest hungers. She calls for us to reintroduce into our vocabulary and fields of conception such time-honored but unpopular (and, among growing numbers of us, quite meaningless) notions as law, sin, vocation, and so on. She invites us to embrace time-honored but often-forgotten ways of being-in-the-world, to cultivate in our lives and communities a *habitus*—a set of dispositions that generate practices, perceptions, and attitudes that are "regular," not governed by "rules"[2]—that is nurtured by and reflective of Jesus' understanding of humanity and his other-centered practices.

This book was not written in a library but hammered out in painful experience, hundreds of therapeutic interactions, and scores of classes and seminars. We need its message.

Joel B. Green, Ph.D.
Associate Professor of New Testament,
American Baptist Seminary of the West
and Graduate Theological Union

Preface

The concept of a psychology emerging from Jesus' life and teachings occurred to me twenty years ago when I was in seminary. I had enrolled at Pacific School of Religion in Berkeley, my hometown, in order to develop my counseling skills formally so that I would be better equipped to work with the high school students I was teaching at the time. I studied pastoral psychology and the Bible side by side. Pastoral psychology, at that time mostly humanistic, was exciting, but it did not measure up to either the inspiration provided to me by my mentors or the spirit of the seminary community. Because of these gaps in my formal training as a psychologist, I was continually attracted to something in the life of Jesus that came closer to my own understanding of human need and fulfillment. At the time I saw Jesus as a good counselor and observed likenesses between his work and the work of therapists writing in the 1970s.

I eventually changed careers from high school teacher to licensed marriage and family counselor and worked with many seminarians, ministers, and church people. Biblical stories came naturally to mind; we used them as life metaphors in the therapeutic process. Then one spring a local church invited me to teach a Lenten series. In the process of preparing my lectures, it suddenly occurred to me that through my studies and counseling I had pieced together a practical psychology based upon the Gospel stories. That Lenten series began the project that has culminated in this book. The ideas presented here evolved within a series of communities where fertile conversation continues: the seminary community, the counseling office, and the classroom. The entire process has been guided by the Spirit of God.

Writing the book itself has been a community experience and I want to thank the many people who have become a part of this project. First, for nearly twenty years I have been privileged to be a part of the intimate community formed between therapist and client. I am grateful to those individuals who have shared their stories with me and have graciously allowed me to retell them in these pages (I have used pseudonyms in these situations). The adult class at Epworth United Methodist Church in Berkeley that asked me to teach the initial Lenten series, "Psychology of Jesus," in 1985 provided the inspiration and opportunity to get this book started. My own church, Montclair Presbyterian Church in Oakland, most particularly my prayer partners, Carol Ekberg and Candyce Rennegarbe, offered more opportunities to teach and nurtured me through these years. The excellent community of New College for Advanced Christian Studies in Berkeley, both colleagues and students, have provided vital support. Joel Green, New Testament professor and dean at New College during much of this process, has not only guided my use of the New Testament, read many drafts, and written the foreword, but originally hired me to teach "Resurrection Psychology" in 1988. I owe much to Karen Hernandez, herself a psychotherapist and a member of my first graduate-level class, who insisted, indeed demanded, that I begin writing. My excellent research assistant, Bonnie Howe, scholar and writer herself, a graduate of New College, pursued references, adjusted footnotes, called my attention to overused words, discussed content, and offered suggestions. Ever a support, my spiritual director, Frank Houdek, S.J., not only encouraged my progress but also introduced me to Loyola University Press. Joseph Downey, S.J., warmly welcomed me to that community, and Jeremy Langford accompanied me in preparing the manuscript.

Herman Waetjen, New Testament scholar, aided my early use of the New Testament and taught "Resurrection Psychology and Gospel Story" with me at Pacific School of

Religion in 1989. Readers have been legion; two were in it for the long haul, Max Lopez-Cepero and Barbara Bennett, who read drafts, offered suggestions, and edited the text. A final thanks to my husband, Donald Alter, who is always my primary source of support.

Introduction

On the whole, I do not find Christians, outside of the catacombs, sufficiently sensible of conditions. Does anyone have the foggiest idea what sort of power we so blithely invoke? Or, as I suspect, does no one believe a word of it? The churches are children playing on the floor with their chemistry sets, mixing up a batch of TNT to kill a Sunday morning. It is madness to wear ladies' straw hats and velvet hats to church; we should all be wearing crash helmets. Ushers should issue life preservers and signal flares, they should lash us to our pews. For the sleeping god may wake someday and take offense, or the waking god may draw us out to where we can never return (Dillard 1982, 40–41).

Christianity is both radical and ridiculous, and no matter how we try to tame it through our familiarity, Jesus the Astonishing and the Beloved, stands in the midst of Scripture turning the world upside down, turning our world upside down. Are we, as Annie Dillard suggests in the passage above, failing to be "sufficiently sensible of conditions?" Do we really grasp the essence of liturgy and song or Gospel and sermon? Do we realize the appalling power that we invoke? Week by week, Sunday by Sunday, Bible study by Bible study, Eucharist by Eucharist, we celebrate awesome mystery. We tell a story we can only partly grasp. We live our lives in memory of One raised from the dead. We claim and believe that the Resurrection, this astonishing foolishness, shapes and sustains the way we live our lives.

Human language strains into metaphor and symbol trying to explain, or at least describe, that which appears through the vision of biblical writers. Saint Paul warned us that it would all appear foolish, and indeed there is no way around it. It does. And perhaps nowhere has the majesty of Christian truth looked more foolish than as described by the silver tongue and impeccable logic of Sigmund Freud. Considering the claim that religious experience produced an "oceanic feeling" and working with solid confidence in intellectual objectivity, Freud wrote:

> After all, a feeling can only be a source of energy if it is itself the expression of a strong need. The derivation of religious needs from the infant's helplessness and the longing for the father aroused by it seems to me incontrovertible, especially since the feeling is not simply prolonged from childhood days, but is permanently sustained by fear of the superior power of Fate. . . . The origin of the religious attitude can be traced back in clear outlines as far as the feeling of infantile helplessness (1961, 19).

Scholarly consideration of faith has never recovered from Freud's attack. In the United States, Psychology of Religion, which began in the 1880s as a study of normal adulthood, completely vanished as an area of respectable scholarship by 1930 only to emerge shyly in the 1970s after humanism had chiseled away the mystique of "objective scientific inquiry" (Beit-Hallahmi 1977, 17–26). In more recent years the two fields, psychology and faith, have begun tentative approaches toward one another. These have often occurred through the friendliness of particular psychological theorists like Jung or Frankl, believers themselves, who include a dimension of faith in their understanding of human personality.

What I propose for this book is more radical. I want to approach as psychology what we celebrate in Sunday worship, the divine foolishness of Jesus in the gospel stories taken at face value. I explore the practical psychology that Jesus employed as he taught, healed, and encountered people of his day. Since these stories, the four Gospels, come to us as the church's post-resurrection remembrances of Jesus' ministry, the power of Easter is implied in their telling. As I use them to explore how Jesus understood human need and fulfillment, I also assume the brooding presence of God who at Easter defeated the deepest of human terrors. Hence, I take my title, *Resurrection Psychology,* from the most incomprehensible event of the entire Christian mystery.

Resurrection Psychology is a practical understanding of human personality observable in Jesus' life and teachings. It centers on a few basic assumptions about human need, personal fulfillment, and social good that are played out in a variety of emphases in the stories of the four Gospels. Together these create a system, something like a personality theory. Much of Jesus' psychological system overlaps contemporary psychology and confirms current research findings. In some cases it either departs from or flatly challenges particular psychological assumptions. And in still other instances, Jesus' assumptions about human need and fulfillment are different from those discussed in psychology, and his system adds unexpected, sometimes startling, dimensions to our understanding of human personality. In many places his practical psychology, like his parabolic teaching, is paradoxical.

My purpose in this book is to explore Jesus' basic assumptions by examining closely ten aspects of his system as they appear in gospel stories. I reflect on their significance for understanding and helping human beings, and observe their consistence with or divergence from currently accepted theories of psychology. In the process I will draw upon stories from individual lives to illustrate what we observed in psychological theory and in the gospel accounts.

Two basic assumptions underlie Jesus' understanding of human beings and must be noted from the beginning in order to put the system in perspective. First, Jesus assumes the presence of a God of the universe, one who is in love with humanity and remains intensely interested and available. Second, Jesus assumes that all human beings are burdened with a need for forgiveness. These two assumptions, markedly

different from what we in the West have understood in the
study of human personality, permeate every aspect of Jesus'
approach to human need, fulfillment, and social good: his
emphasis on forgiveness, his understanding of law, his resistance to humanity's fear-driven need to control in its many
forms, his call to and method of concern for others, as well as
his definition of psychological evil and a method for its defeat.

The first of these assumptions, God's abiding interested
love, provides a foundation for Jesus' understanding of human
need and fulfillment. It arises from a strikingly different world
view. Marcus Borg has pointed out that Jesus' world, unlike
our current Western culture, took the reality of the Spirit seriously and literally. "What Jesus was, historically speaking, was
a Spirit-filled person in the charismatic stream of Judaism. . . .
In an important sense, all that he was, taught, and did flowed
out of his own intimate experience of the 'world of Spirit'"
(1987, 25). Hence, his understanding of human personality is
embedded in this experience.

The second assumption, universal human need for forgiveness, underlies many gospel interactions. Jesus continually
notes a lingering burden in the consciousness of those around
him, and time after time he responds with enthusiastic decla-
rations of forgiveness. If Jesus offers forgiveness to those
seeking healing, he also confronts the "righteous" with their
need for forgiveness. These together represent a consistent
theme, an attitude, that pervades the gospel accounts. This
second emphasis, as well, is problematic in the West. If one
were to ask Jesus, "Forgiveness for what?" he would certainly
say, "for your sins." And people in Western culture, children
of the Enlightenment with its condescending attitude toward
faith, have long ago ceased believing in sin. For the most part,
clinicians believe the concept of sin itself has instilled in
believing persons a chronic neurotic guilt and shame. Even
Karl Menninger's 1973 protest book *What Ever Became of Sin?*
did not successfully convince the therapeutic world to recon-
sider the power of the term *sin*. I would like, then, to persuade the reader to attend to theologian Paul Tillich's caution
not to dispose of the great words of Christianity too quickly.
Embedded in Jesus' tender and insistent forgiveness lies an

important understanding of chronic human need, which we explore thoroughly in chapter 1.

Jesus' two basic assumptions will manifest themselves in many ways throughout this study. The rest of the material clusters in different ways. First, since it is important to elaborate Jesus' understanding of the place of forgiveness in human life, we need also to consider his assertion of the importance of law: tender acceptance on one hand, and strenuous command on the other. In chapter 2 we consider the place of "law" in psychology as an essential psychological component for establishing boundaries, living within limits, and becoming a compassionate self. Then we observe how Jesus returned the law to its essential intent by teaching an enacted redemptive love that promotes quality living not only for the community, but for all people. Truly the people of God become a blessing to the world. The law which Jesus describes awakens us to hope and love as if the Kingdom of God were fully present.

Jesus has a great deal to say about human passion for control as a basic resistance to the vulnerability of finitude. Semiconscious, if conscious at all, human desire for control masquerades as a bid for safety. I suggest that it is essentially an unconscious resistance to finiteness, masking a fear of death or a panic over insignificance. In chapter 3 we explore crushing, fear-driven control as it operates in perfectionistic striving and compare it with Jesus' invitation into another way of being. In chapter 4 we examine the paradoxical death of control required in order to embody the image of God within us. In other words, by relinquishing desperate acts to control, we enter into received holiness and personal peace.

Unquestionably, Jesus calls human beings into concern for others, and arguably such concern contributes to psychological health. Human longing for control, however, often interferes with service to others. In chapter 5 we explore Jesus' method of healing through activating responsibility—that is, the ability to respond—as an essential component in empowering human living. We will also consider the place in spiritual development where fearful controlling interrupts continued development and derails empowering helpfulness. In chapter 6 we investigate Jesus' style of psychology, his paradoxical method of disrupting control so that human beings might become vulnerable enough to give and receive blessing. In chapter 7 we examine the psychological influence on the sense of value in human life as Jesus' call to concern becomes life's vocation.

If resistance to finitude and its attendant need to control interferes with personal peace and concern for others, it also disrupts our ability to read our own feelings. In chapter 8 we consider disruptive internal voices, which operate much like ancient prophets and cry out against the status quo in our own lives or in the community. Although Jesus clearly operates from his embodied prophetic perspective, many Christians have worked to stifle their own prophetic voices in the name of Christian maturity. When released from our own fearful stranglehold, these voices become prophetic messengers highlighting urgent issues for ourselves, for our communities, and for the world.

I have described Jesus' consistent disruption of human longing to control as he seeks to bring human beings into fuller and more compassionate lives. In chapter 9 I look directly at psychological evil as it relates to control and at Jesus' admonition not to resist evil. Evil is part of life and, as such, it has its consequences: it causes damage and it leaves scars. In chapter 10 we explore the paradoxical significance of scars in light of the Resurrection. In the post-Resurrection accounts it was not Jesus' eloquence but his scars and suffering that made him credible. In the same way, human beings need not despair over the scars that identify them. It is precisely these scars that God transforms into ultimate good for those who bear them and for the enhanced ability to offer compassionate ministry to others.

Resurrection Psychology, therefore, addresses the worst that life might bring. Personal confidence lies not in preventing anything bad from happening, nor in seeking perfect healing of psychological wounds, but rather in the transforming power of God promised through the Resurrection of Jesus Christ.

Centrality of Forgiveness

P articipants in a church adult education class had no trouble identifying with characters in the story we were using. Like most biblical accounts, the story of the paralytic in Mark 2 introduces universal human themes. Inviting the class to close their eyes, I read the story aloud. Jesus was teaching in Capernaum when four townspeople carried to him a paralyzed man. Realizing they could not get close to Jesus because of the crowd, the four dug through the roof of the house and lowered the mat on which their friend lay. "When Jesus saw their faith, he said to the paralytic, 'Son, your sins are forgiven'" (Mk 2:5). When the reading was finished, I invited class members to find some paralysis in their own lives, some area of concern against which they have made little progress. I asked them to imagine friends and family surrounding them with concern, trying to help and eventually persuading them to try bringing the paralysis to this healer Jesus. I instructed them to imagine the healing experience right through to Jesus' parting challenge: "I say to you, stand up, take your mat and go to your home" (Mk 2:11).

It was a meditative exercise that could have taken an hour or a weekend, not just the five minutes allotted during our forty-five-minute class time. When I called participants back from their reflections, I asked some questions to invite them to share their experiences: What was it like to be forgiven and healed? How was it to have friends and family so concerned?

How did you feel facing Jesus, when he told you to get up and walk? Responses varied: "It was scary," "I couldn't look at him," "It felt good to have my friends care," "I didn't believe Jesus could just heal me so quickly," "I wanted my family and friends to just leave me alone in my misery," "I was so hopeful and so apprehensive," "I was ashamed to let him see me that way." One person said, "I wasn't sure that I wanted to be healed."

The paralyzed man's story itself raised important questions: "Why," one man asked, "did Jesus pronounce forgiveness first?" "Yes," agreed a second class member, "I thought this was a healing story. What has forgiveness to do with healing?"

"It is even an odd sort of forgiveness," I observed. "He doesn't ask the paralytic to confess. Repentance is assumed. And Jesus seems so eager, as if he's lifting a terrible burden. In another rendering of this story, in Matthew 9, he says, 'Take heart, son; your sins are forgiven'" (Mt 9:2).

"It is as though," one woman reflected, "Jesus presupposes the paralytic is more burdened by sin than by paralysis. If we put ourselves in his place, perhaps Jesus infers that about us." "I don't like this sin stuff," the first speaker commented with frustration. "I'm not sure what it means. I wish Jesus hadn't used the word *sin*."

The story stirred much comment and reflection. Although a story of healing, Jesus pronounces forgiveness before doing anything else as though the hidden burden of sin were the real problem. If we were to follow Jesus through the pages of the Gospels, we would find many forgiveness stories combined with other issues. The word *forgiveness* appears many times, but even when it does not appear, Jesus' actions often indicate forgiveness. We might even say that Jesus assumes a forgiving posture as he engages in his ministry. It is as though a primary tenet in his practical understanding of psychology is that human beings are burdened with a need to be forgiven. His ministry, therefore, is unmistakably marked by a centrality of forgiveness.

The quality of Jesus' forgiveness is also unusual. He appears so convinced of this universal human burden that he does not seem to require people to repent or confess wrongdoing. Indeed, he does not need to place blame, even in situations where an individual is obviously at fault. His forgiveness, rather, stems from an inclusive acceptance, an unconditional positive valuing of a particular individual.[1] It is as though what he said of Jerusalem, he means also for us: he would gather us to him as a hen gathers her chicks (Mt 23:37, Lk 13:34). His manner of forgiveness is personal and tender; he creates community inclusively in forgiveness rather than defining community by excluding those who do not conform.[2] Ironically, Jesus' harsh confrontations are reserved only for those who form community exclusively by careful attention to the holiness codes.

Throughout his ministry, Jesus insisted on the human need for God's forgiveness. Consequently, I have chosen to make God's forgiveness my emphasis here, instead of focusing on our own forgiveness of others, which is the more prevalent concern in most churches where I teach. By his insistence that we need to receive God's forgiveness, Jesus perceives an element of basic human need and acts to minister to it. In moments of reflection it is not hard to recognize the significance of his insight.

But forgiveness itself implies that we humans need forgiveness from something. And that something is one of most difficult of all Christian words: *sin.* One adult class member spoke for many of us by saying, "I don't like this sin stuff." And indeed the "sin stuff" of Christian theology is a problem for our contemporary world—a world steeped in psychological assumptions about human goodness and practically unlimited potential. While psychologists have their own way of addressing human evil, most resist Christianity's assertion that human beings, universally, are sinful. Therefore, in order to bring together Christianity and psychology, we must somehow deal with this basic concept. Theologian Paul Tillich has argued that great Christian words like *sin* and *grace,* though distorted through misuse, cannot be replaced. Rather, he claims, they must be redefined for every generation:

> I should like to suggest another word to you, not as a substitute for the word "sin," but as a useful clue in interpretation of the word "sin": "separation." Separation is an aspect of the experience of everyone. Perhaps the word

"sin" has the same root as the word "asunder." In any case, *sin is separation*. To be in the state of sin is to be in the state of separation (1948, 154).

Tillich asserts that sin is a state of being before it is an action. Sin is a state of being separated from oneself, from others, and from the Ground of Our Being. Tillich reminds us that "we not only suffer with other creatures because of the self-destructive consequences of our separation, but also know *why* we suffer. We know that we are estranged from something to which we really belong and with which we *should* be united" (ibid., 155). Since "separation" holds a positive connotation in clinical psychology that deals with becoming a mature adult, I would alter Tillich's phrase to more closely approach the way he intended it in the 1940s: Sin is a state of being alienated from oneself, from others, and from God. It is universal, a part of existence itself, and we all participate in it. Within our alienation we experience loss, emptiness, and shame. And out of our sense of alienation, we behave in alienating ways. The deeper our alienation, the deeper our shame and the more vicious our treatment of others.

Jesus' manner of forgiveness is inclusive, community restoring. He returns those he forgives to themselves, to the community, and to God. Confident that we all need forgiveness and that alienation devastates our lives, Jesus, who is tender with the guilty, harshly confronts the good religious people who have chosen separation from others by means of strict adherence to conventional codes of purity.

We have observed Jesus' manner of forgiveness in a healing story, but let us examine this characteristic in other settings. The story of Zacchaeus (Lk 19:1–10) is a forgiveness story, though the word *forgiveness* is never used. Zacchaeus, we are told, is a rich tax collector. By this we know that he works for the Romans and that he probably charges more than is required so he can pad his own pockets. Zacchaeus is, therefore, perceived as a traitor to his own people, alienated from them by his own actions. He is undoubtedly excluded from community and most certainly from the intimacy of table fellowship.[3] Zacchaeus's status in the community is already indicated by the behavior of the crowd: as a rule "People of reputation, of status, are granted a view by others, irrespective of their height" (Green 1994, 20). But Zacchaeus, a short man, is forced to climb a sycamore tree in order to see Jesus as he passes through town. Zacchaeus is an outcast.

In addition to his own exclusion, any people seen associating with Zacchaeus were considered tainted as well. It is no wonder, then, that the crowd begins to grumble when Jesus invites himself to dinner at Zacchaeus's house. A surprising behavior in our culture, this self-invitation constituted an act of profoundly intimate inclusion in the first-century Jewish society. Jesus returns Zacchaeus to the community through his own person, with table fellowship serving as a dramatic act of inclusive forgiveness. Zacchaeus responds as if forgiven; he repents and radically departs from his alienating behavior. The forgiveness is offered; repentance connects him with it. Jesus concludes with a joyful pronouncement: "Today salvation has come to this house, because this too is a son of Abraham" (Lk 19:9). In other words, "Zacchaeus also is one of us."

In another story, Jesus is confronted by a crowd of people who push before them a guilty woman, caught, we are told, "in the very act of adultery" (Jn 8:1–11). The woman is profoundly alienated. There is no one to protect her or to take her side. No one accompanies her, and no one comes forward to offer her support. Not even the woman's partner with whom she committed adultery appears. In this scenario, she is treated as an object in the hands of her captors. Perhaps this unprotected woman has been known to engage in sexual liaisons before, a safe object to use for testing Jesus. No one will question her guilt. Possibly, like many victims of sexual abuse, she has no confidence to refuse sexual overtures. But Jesus assumes that all have sinned, all are in need of forgiveness. The men ask him if he affirms the law and agrees that the woman should be stoned; Jesus simply refuses to answer. We are told that Jesus writes with his fingers on the ground. But the men act with the certainty of the law on their side, and they press the issue: "What do you say?" It was the wrong question; Jesus confronts them with their hypocrisy: "Let anyone among you who is without sin be the first to throw a stone at her." He insists on the universal need for forgiveness and returns again to his writing. The men leave. Jesus has opened a healing possibility to them. Now that they too acknowledge their alienation, their sin, they also can rejoin the human community.

Then, when Jesus is left alone with the woman, we see again the unusual quality of his forgiveness: personal, tender, understated—an unconditional positive valuing. The forgiveness relieves the woman's burden and her shame. But Jesus, whose forgiveness has that personal quality, offers her an additional protection, the right to refuse repeated sexual abuse. Through his injunction—"Go on your way, and from now on do not sin again"—he empowers her to say no where it has been impossible before.[4]

Jesus is convinced that human beings languish in their need for forgiveness. No matter how obviously guilty or no matter how righteously self-justified they are, Jesus seeks to return human beings to themselves, to their communities, and to God. No individual is too deeply alienated—not Zacchaeus, traitor to his people, nor the woman caught "in the very act of adultery." Jesus meets these people in their suffering with forgiveness. But Jesus' compassion extends beyond the obviously shamed and shameful. He seeks to expose the denied shame buried in a disguise of self-righteousness. He is convinced that no individual is sufficiently self-justified to alleviate this human burden alone. Through parable and confrontation, Jesus holds a mirror before the fragile self-defense of the righteous just as he did with the woman's accusers. In this way he opens an approach for ending their alienation and bringing about their inclusion and return to a different sense of community, to themselves, and to God.

When we consider this basic tenet in Jesus' practical understanding of human psychology, we find it very much in keeping with the clinical experience of counselors. Indeed without forgiveness, very much as Jesus embodied it, we human beings are psychologically chained to the past. The drinking man continues to drink, the overeating woman continues to sneak food, the lying child continues to lie. Behavior becomes hidden, shame-filled, compulsive, driving the individual deeper and deeper into isolation, fear, and self-loathing. Out of control, we struggle to achieve control not only of ourselves but of others, lest they might see us for who we are. In response to our isolation, we lash out, take offense, find fault. Without community we are desperate, hostile, and dangerous.

It is Jesus' model of exposing the hidden and receiving the wounded that restores the lost to community and to health. A foundational tenet of family therapy highlights the same wisdom: there is no innocent party or guilty party. When a family is troubled, all members participate. A similar wisdom has been employed by Alcoholics Anonymous. It is precisely compassionate connection as embodied forgiveness that is central to all therapeutic work.

A life story helps illustrate this point. Catherine and George sought help when they found their fights had become intensely painful and futile. They were no longer able to argue issues through to a satisfactory conclusion. As they presented their struggle, they agreed that George was "a very nice guy" and that Catherine's bursts of temper were placing tremendous stress on their family. Catherine protested that she did not feel George listened to her, but she too was puzzled and upset by her outbursts. Taken at face value, Catherine was clearly the problem.

A few months before they came to see me, an incident took place that alienated Catherine from George's family and caused them both considerable pain. As the holidays approached, it was clear that Catherine had no intention of attending any of George's family gatherings. During the summer, Catherine had planned activities for their two children so that she could have two peaceful weeks in order to catch up with the details of the small family business she ran from an office in their home. About that time George's sister called to say that she and her family were planning to visit the San Francisco Bay Area and would like to stay with them. "By all means," said easy-going George. "In fact, the kids are in camp those weeks. Catherine will be free."

Catherine, who tended to be very conscientious, felt criticized by George's sister. "I lasted about ten days," she reported, "and then I blew." George was astonished. He could not understand Catherine's burst of temper, and he felt deeply hurt by the rift in the family. Catherine was devastated and was completely unable to explain her tension to George.

From an observer's perspective, there is no mystery about the problem. Catherine's explosive response initially threatened to disguise the fact that George's behavior exacerbated the stress. George was clearly an easy-going, thoroughly nice human being. But George was also sweetly unconscious of Catherine's needs and priorities, and cheerfully undermined her plans by neglecting to check signals with her. By the time he had said yes to his sister, Catherine could only take the role of the shrew. Caught between her initial plans and suddenly playing the role of family hostess because of George's decision, Catherine accepted the visit but was unable to endure the stress.

In working with this couple, I needed to embody forgiveness to Catherine for her obvious participation in the family pain. Much as Jesus understood the suffering that our alienating actions thrust upon us, I needed to understand the pain and humiliation Catherine's bursts of anger inflicted upon her. With George I needed to hold an insistent mirror before his cheerful insensitivity. This was also in keeping with Jesus' basic understanding of the human dilemma. There is no way to be comfortably righteous in relation to, separate from, and uncontaminated by guilty others. All are burdened with a need for forgiveness. Those who are aware of the burden must be received and those who are unaware must be awakened.

Jesus clearly places his finger on a central psychological issue by emphasizing the human need for forgiveness. My adult church school class had no trouble identifying in themselves "paralyzed" spots, hidden within themselves and deeply troubling. These areas that are out of our control shame us and make us feel small, lost, and burdened. Secret knowledge of ourselves makes us self-conscious. American humorist Garrison Keillor quipped, "We always have a backstage view of ourselves." Our secret self-consciousness makes us hesitant to recognize inner struggle in other people who seem "so normal." Certainly Jesus' insistent compassion hits a nerve, but what exactly does he recognize that is such a universal human dilemma even today?

Jesus' insistent focus on the need for forgiveness highlights a largely secret plight in human living that isolates and paralyzes us; that is, shame. As Gershen Kaufman explains:

> To feel shame is to feel *seen* in a painfully diminished sense. The self feels exposed both to itself and to anyone else present. It is this sudden, unexpected feeling of expo-

sure and accompanying self-consciousness that character-izes the essential nature of the affect of shame. Contained in the experience of shame is the piercing awareness of ourselves as fundamentally deficient in some vital way as a human being. To live with shame is to experience the very essence or heart of the self as wanting.

Shame is an impotence-making experience because it *feels* as *though* there is no way to relieve the matter, no way to restore the balance of things. One has simply failed as a human being. No single action is seen as wrong and, hence, reparable (1985, 8).

In Kaufman's description, shame's tendency to overwhelm and isolate becomes apparent. It cancels one's self: it is not so much what we have *done* as what we *are*. Ray Mitchell adds to our understanding of this phenomenon: "Gradually shame can become internalized to such an extent that it becomes an autonomous phenomenon which is resistant even to contra-dicting external stimuli" (1989, 107). Once internalized, recur-rence of shame is inevitable. Mitchell concludes his review of research literature on shame with the observation that shame is ubiquitous and universal: "To be human then, is to live inti-mately with shame" (ibid., 100).

I suggest that Jesus' recurring focus on forgiveness arises from his awareness of this universal phenomenon. He intends to step between an individual and self-crippling, alienating shame. Jesus meets each individual at his or her point of in-tense shame. We are indeed seen and known, but he draws us into God's love and cancels our alienation through forgive-ness: "Son, your sins are forgiven"; "Zacchaeus . . . I must stay at your house today"; "Neither do I condemn you. Go your way, and from now on do not sin again." For those who would deny their shame through adherence to an elaborate system of laws and codes, Jesus has another message: "You must repent."

But we in the Western world have an essentially shameless culture. That is, we do not advocate using shame to control. In fact, unlike our counterparts in many parts of the world, we generally avoid using shame in socializing children. We choose to raise our children to be bold and independent. We are more likely to believe in our children's nearly unlimited potential and encourage them to develop broadly rather than to expect adherence to duty, respect, and responsibility. Indeed two generations of parents in the United States have been strongly discouraged from using shaming techniques. We have been directed to listen reflectively, to correct or praise a child's behavior without reference to a child's character. Although the recognition of shame as a shaping force has diminished in American culture, the actual occurrence of shame persists and often without awareness of its true nature.

Mitchell asserts that shame often persists without recognition and without a name. He indicates that shame attaches itself to other feelings and becomes formless to such a degree that it is hard to recognize. Only women, who are more likely to be socialized for cooperation with others, may still be able to recognize shame, but the study of shame in the male-dominated field of psychology has been neglected.

Why does shame persist in a culture that does not utilize it? Where does shame come from? When the topic of shame has been addressed in psychology, it has been cited largely in the context of the family. Much clinical and virtually all popular literature suggests that shame and guilt are the fault of damaging interpersonal relationships. For example, families suffering from excessive stress, which can be produced by such things as poverty, alcoholism, domestic violence, or child abuse, tend to produce children who experience intense, crippling shame.[5] Likewise, adults who remember specific instances of feeling shamed by angry parents often lead lives that are shadowed by feelings of inadequacy. Shame, once internalized from these interpersonal experiences, self-help sources assert, may be acted out in a variety of disguises—violence, shyness, or anorexia. The acting out itself distracts from the essential devastating feeling of shame: terrified lostness, worthlessness, or emptiness.

The problem of shame is much more complicated and its occurrence much more universal than many theorists and popularizers have acknowledged. Further investigation reveals that even in families where a child is not abused or verbally shamed, children may absorb family tension and somehow blame themselves for it. It becomes increasingly apparent that shame exists even in families where there is no unusual stress: no alcoholism, no particular violence, and no child abuse. But let us briefly review psychology's proposals for shame's etiology.

Until recently, most understandings of shame have indicated that it begins in an interpersonal setting.[6] Harry Stack Sullivan, who first described psychological development as an interpersonal phenomenon, observed that infants automatically split the self into three parts: good me, bad me, and not me. Sullivan described "not me," a part of the self so steeped in shame that it is split off from conscious awareness, as developing in the relationship between infant and mother, most particularly because of the mother's acute anxiety over a particular aspect of the child's behavior. Genital exploration, for example, might be rapidly curtailed or suppressed by the mother's horrified response (Sullivan 1953, 161–64). Erik Erikson also understood shame as a social issue, but he concluded that it occurred around toilet training experiences and human struggle between autonomy and external control (1963, 251). Heinz Kohut, through his work with shame-laden narcissistic patients, proposed that shame occurs when a child receives insufficient response from a mothering person (Baker and Baker 1987). When a mother is too preoccupied or simply resistant to mothering, her ability to sufficiently "mirror," or respond to, overtures from a toddler or young child is significantly diminished. The child experiences this indifference with shame: "I am not good enough to be interesting to my mother. If I were somehow different, mother would be fascinated." Alice Miller popularized this idea with her book *The Drama of the Gifted Child,* depicting openly hostile mothers who saw their children as something to be trained (1981).

This idea certainly corroborated understandings of human development put forth by attachment theorists, Ainsworth (1978) and Bowlby (1988), who suggested that all human security begins with attachment to a mothering person. Laboratory findings from the infant research of Daniel Stern also indicate the enormous importance of bonding between mother and infant. In observing mothers and infants playing together, Stern found that mothers tended to make noises or body movements that replicated noises initiated by the child. When the mother's response failed to match the child's utterance, the child seemed startled. Stern asserts that when a child repeatedly fails to elicit a matched response or when a child simply is unable to attract mother's attention, the child internalizes the lack of response as a personal failure (1985).

Ainsworth, Bowlby, Stern, and Miller all imply that proper parenting would eliminate shame. Shame is understood as developing exclusively in an interpersonal setting through the failure of a nurturing environment. All of this is frightening news to parents, particularly mothers, who bear an enormous responsibility in these theories for the development of shame. Nevertheless, it is apparent that children who are securely attached, doted on in early life by moms, protected, nurtured, and carefully schooled, also demonstrate troubling occurrences of shame. While not to diminish the power we mothers unwittingly wield with our children, shame is more basic to human personality and development than anything a human parent can anticipate or control. Even the occurrence of shame in an interpersonal setting takes unpredictable turns.

Citing the work of two researchers, Francis Broucek observes that after an infant, at about four months of age, can distinguish the face of its mother from other faces, the baby will respond with cognitive shock and shame (shyness) when a stranger approaches. Indeed, even an infant's mother absorbed in her own thoughts or conflicts can appear as a stranger to the infant and inadvertently induce a shame reaction. Broucek writes:

> I reviewed a number of experimental studies which dealt with the infant's control over environmental events and his attendant joy in recreating events contingent on his activity. These studies also revealed a corresponding acute distress state associated with the inability to influence, predict, or comprehend an event which the infant expected, on the basis of previous experiences, to be able to control or understand. The descriptions of the behavioral and physiological characteristics of certain of these infantile "distress" states suggest a primitive shame experience (1982).

If Broucek is right, shame occurs for children in social settings when their anticipated control over the situation exceeds their ability to enact that control. Shame arises from disap-

pointment of designs to influence or control. Such disappoint-
ments carry an element of cognitive shock.

Mitchell employs Broucek's description of cognitive shock
as causing shame when he describes a two-year-old boy who
had just learned to appreciate the concept of wholeness eagerly anticipating receiving a cookie. When the cookie offered
happens to be broken, he responds with rage (Mitchell 1989,
57). Mitchell indicates that the cognitive shock inherent in
failed expectation elicits a flood of shame. Silvan S. Tomkins, a
theorist of human feelings or affect, writes, "Shame is inevitable for any human being insofar as desire outruns fulfillment sufficiently to attenuate interest without destroying it"
(1963, 185).

If, indeed, shame occurs through failed parenting, there is
cause for self-righteous indignation and vigorous effort to control its occurrence. But if, in fact, we are observing shame as
desire outrunning fulfillment, we are facing a stunning theological issue. Shame-inducing overreaching makes its first appearance on the heels of creation. In Genesis 3, Adam and Eve
strive to be "like God, knowing good and evil" (Gn 3:5) and
spontaneously experience shame. Jesus apparently assumes
this excess when he faces the paralyzed young man or as he
welcomes Zacchaeus back into human community. Desire that
has exceeded social convention was obvious for the woman
caught in adultery, yet Jesus tenderly refuses to condemn her. I
propose that human beings routinely overreach and that
shame is ubiquitous. Current research supports this position.

Robert Karen, summarizing contemporary therapeutic emphasis on shame for the *Atlantic Monthly,* writes, ". . . shame
is suddenly everywhere in the literature and is seen by some
as 'the master emotion,' the unseen regulator of our entire af-
fective life" (1992). While Karen cites parental failure as the
source of shame, three theorists who would understand
shame as "the master emotion" do not agree that shame begins interpersonally. Silvan Tomkins understands affect including shame as a basic part of human biology:

> I see affect of feeling as *the primary innate biological
> motivating mechanism,* more urgent than drive depriva-
> tion and pleasure, and more urgent even than physical

pain. Without its amplification, nothing else matters, and with its amplification anything can matter. It thus combines urgency, abstractness, and generality (1987, 137).

Tomkins understands shame as a control mechanism used to modify an excitement-joy response. That is, when human beings feel overtaken by either excitement or joy, they are likely to restore their sense of control through spontaneously employing shame. Donald Nathanson endorses Tomkins: "Since affect theory assumes that the affects are subcortical mechanisms, and that they have always existed in the 'reptile brain' (MacLean, 1975, p. 214), I think it unlikely that shame (or any affect for that matter) is produced by a very complex mechanism" (1987, 25). He adds a biological note: individuals indicate the existence of neurological or chemical components to shame by responding differently to the same stimulus. He suggests that the shame response is so painful that sufferers will search through a "card catalog" of their experience to find an incident that matches the pain. These researchers clearly challenge the assumptions of popular culture that imply that shame should be alien to "normal" adulthood. The occurrence of shame becomes a much more complicated issue.[7]

In Nathanson's description of shame, he offers examples from settings that are both social and individual:

> Whenever the organism is required to break off enjoyment-joy in a situation in which it wants to maintain the enjoyment, shame affect may be recruited to turn off enjoyment-joy in a manner analogous to the action of shame as a reducer of interest-excitement. Thus, when we commune with another person, this mutual enjoyment is a major force in socialization. But if we realize suddenly that our partner is no longer enjoying what had been a shared joke, we may turn away in shame (ibid., 22).

This example demonstrates an incident of shame that reflects the findings of Ainsworth, Bowlby, Stern, and Miller, but Nathanson recognizes shame as more far-reaching:

> I have observed a 10-month-old become fascinated by a shiny bracelet, look to his mother for permission to in-

spect it, then do so with growing interest and excitement, and finally (responding to an unknown stimulus), tear himself away from his involvement with this wonderful object only with great difficulty *by covering his face with his hands and turning his head.* This form of shyness may be the innate affect shame functioning to reduce interest-excitement (ibid., 23).

In other words, the infant is overtaken with excitement beyond his control. To regain control, he uses shame to dampen his excitement.

Jerome Kagan, in his 1984 *The Nature of the Child,* cites another example of shame in his discussion of the child's development of performance standards. He suggests that it is not so much an event that brings about intensely bad feelings, but the interpretation devised in the child:

A third source of standards emerges when the child realizes that he can or cannot attain a goal through use of his talents. Two-year-olds become very upset if they are unable to meet a standard for mastery imposed by another person. When a woman approaches a child [in a laboratory setting], picks up some toys, acts out some brief sequences that are difficult to remember or to implement, then returns to her chair, children from diverse cultural settings will immediately cry or protest. . . . It is unlikely that these children had been punished for failing to imitate either their parents or another adult. . . . I believe that the child invents an obligation to duplicate the adult's actions and, additionally, knows that she is unable to do so (1984, 127).

Again, we are observing shame induced by the child's own sense of inadequacy in the face of a task that he has decided he should be able to perform. In this case the experience of inadequacy and ensuing shame are tied to development.

Shame is a painful emotion that threatens to cancel our sense of self. It sweeps over our lives at moments when we feel suddenly out of control or when we have overstepped our ability. It occurs at moments when we feel exposed to others or to ourselves. While it is amplified in families that suffer from unusual stress or violence, it is apparently universal, innate, and biologically and developmentally influenced. Karen uses the following example, which illustrates this point.

> A mathematics professor in his fifties, who likes to think of himself as dynamic and rakish but who is at the moment "between lovers," stands on the subway platform eyeing an undergraduate. He sees that his gaze is making her uncomfortable. He feels a twinge of shame over this intrusion, but not enough to stop. He files his behavior under "manly aggression" and keeps staring. Then a searing thought enters and exits his mind so fast that later he won't remember having had it. The idea seems almost to have been waiting there like a hot coal, and after stumbling upon it and getting singed, he flees in panic. Feeling inexplicably crestfallen, he looks away from the young woman, buries his head in his paper, and seeks out a separate car when the train comes in. For the rest of the morning he feels listless and down. He doesn't want people near him, and growls if they press. He works methodically, waiting for the unnamable discomfort to pass. The idea that scorched him was an image of himself, all too believable, as a hungry, unhappy loner, a man who had wasted his youth and was incapable of lasting attachments, staring at a woman who could not possibly be interested in him. The shame that the image evoked was too hot to handle (1992).

Shame occurs spontaneously when our fantasy of who we would like to be encounters our "backstage" understanding of who we are.

Shame, as we have already noted, appears early in the Bible. In Genesis 3 human beings overreach themselves in a desire to be in control, and like Karen's mathematics professor, experience shame without external provocation. Adam and Eve's story illustrates ubiquitous human fear of exposure and humiliation; without instigation they seek hiding. It occurs for all human beings, of course, when we seek certain control: "to be like God knowing good and evil." The story in Genesis gives the experience of shame a twist because it represents human resistance to finitude itself, our profound shame in being limited creatures.

It is our inevitable burden of shame that Jesus addresses in his insistent forgiveness. There is no question that shame isolates us from our rejected, "inferior" selves, from others whose sight we fear, and from God whose very existence reminds us of our creatureliness. In our minds we have failed to achieve an inner desire to transcend our finite nature; we have overreached and appeared foolish. We have invented an unnecessary obligation to be as God. As a result, we feel the stinging humiliation of not being good enough, of being inferior and out of control. And, as Mitchell wisely describes, we find faith itself problematic because no matter how kind and benevolent the Divinity is, our shame lies in how greatly we fall short of God's greatness.

But Jesus is the incarnate God who has chosen to limit himself to the status of creature. Jesus approaches us tenderly in our creaturely shame-filled failure, and forgives us our perpetual sin, our longing to be like God, in control of the universe. And God's forgiveness of us is essential because without it we are dangerous. Unless we recognize our own need to be forgiven, forgiveness has a violent underside. Immersed in our own sense of controlled self-righteousness, protected from shame through denial, we hotly oppose forgiveness for those we do not want to forgive. In this case, as in the case of the adulterous woman's accusers, Jesus' forgiveness awakens our searing hidden shame, and we long to rid ourselves of the One Who Forgives.

2

The Necessity of the Law

The small girl ahead of me in the grocery line that Passover season must have been about two-and-a-half years old. She pleaded with her mother to give her the largest box of matzos to carry. As a good parent, the mother squatted down at eye level to talk quietly with her child. She explained that the box, almost the size of the child, was too heavy for the little girl to lift. The mother offered the child a smaller box in substitution. The girl wailed in protest. At last, the mother took the box out of the grocery cart and gave it to the child. And, of course, the box of matzos was too heavy for her, and it slid through her clasped arms to the floor. Immediately the child threw herself on the floor in despair, sobbing inconsolably. The mother then quietly placed the box in the cart, paid for her groceries, picked up her daughter, and left.

When my groceries rolled into check-out, the checker said through her teeth, "I'd like to get my hands on that kid." I did not reply. I felt sorry for the mother. She had been a model of patience. My two children were in high school at the time, but I remembered the early years of potential public humiliation. But being a parent was only one reason for withholding judgment. I was fairly confident that I had within me my own shrieking two-year-old who threatened disintegration when confronted with life's limits. My internal "child" had her own matzo box she wanted to carry. She said things like: "Chocolate chip cookies are *not* fattening!"

Clearly, neither the grocery clerk nor I completely under-stood the drama we just witnessed. We did not recognize that this child had imagined herself grand and unlimited, success-fully lifting the immense box and carrying it triumphantly out of the store. Her defeat was a shame-inducing cognitive shock much like Mitchell's example, cited in the last chapter, in which a two-year-old boy is reduced to shame-filled rage when the whole cookie he had anticipated appeared broken. The child in the store had taken to herself a grandeur that she could not accomplish and the result was crushing humiliation. Certainly in this way the child represents all of us in our human longing to live grandly, graciously, easily beyond lim-its, admired, and applauded, "fulfilling our potential," godlike in our essence.

C. S. Lewis captures a particularly Christian version of this self-appointed grandeur and consequent disappointment in his poem "Pilgrim's Problem." Writing in his later years, he reflects:

> By now I should be entering on the supreme stage
> Of the whole walk, reserved for the late afternoon.

Retaining his walking metaphor, Lewis imagines easy ap-propriation of Christian virtues: temperance, chastity, humility, and fortitude. He concludes:

> I can see nothing like all this. Was the map wrong?
> Maps can be wrong. But the experienced walker knows
> That the other explanation is more often true (1964,
> 119–20).

Law, if we are to understand it in a psychological sense, speaks to us of limits and expectations. Descriptive or pre-scriptive, it sets boundaries around us. The descriptive laws of gravity and metabolism limit our behavior in certain ways. Prescriptive laws like the Ten Commandments bind us in other ways. We can imagine ourselves as grand and gracious, limit-less and beyond parameters that confine others. And the in-evitable confrontation with our limits humiliates us. Yet we are in fact wonderful, and our faith supports that. We are created in the image of God (Gn 1:27), a little less than God (Ps 8:5).

We are wonderful and we are limited, and our limits become a problem to us. One does not successfully defy descriptive laws: gravity or metabolism, and somewhere it has been said that one does not break the Ten Commandments. Rather, breaking commandments breaks us. These basic boundaries on reliable human behavior before God and other human beings are necessary for quality community living. Lying, stealing, murder, idolatry, and adultery are no better for those who do them than they are for the community that suffers as a result.

The reality of human need for the commandments became clear to me in the summer of 1970 while I was working as a volunteer counselor at a drop-in "Rap (conversation or counseling) Center" in Berkeley. It was at the height of the early sexual revolution, when sexual fulfillment was considered an ultimate good. The motto, "if it feels good, do it," was a guiding principle. A young man at the center had just poured out his heart to a group of us, telling us of a "wonderful affair" he had had with a married woman. The affair had continued until he inadvertently fathered a child, whereupon the woman refused to see him again. The woman gave birth, and when the young man protested that he had a right to see his child, she replied, "Just having a little fun in bed doesn't make you a father." He was devastated. At this vulnerable moment in his story, the young man glanced up and spotted a gold cross I wear on a chain around my neck. "Are you a Christian?" he demanded. "Yes," I responded. "Well," he said, "I don't believe all that stuff. Like the Ten Commandments. 'Thou shalt not commit adultery.' I just don't believe it." The law of gravity, the Ten Commandments, each places a limit on our longings. Each limit elicits rage, a sense of being judged, and often shame. Sometimes, like the man from the Rap Center, we will go to great lengths to avoid accepting our limits and facing our mistakes when we overstep our bounds.

Freud observed this collision of individual desire with community requirement:

It was discovered that a person becomes neurotic because he cannot tolerate the amount of frustration which society imposes on him in the service of its cultural ideals, and it was inferred from this that the abolition or reduction of those demands would result in a return to possibilities of happiness (1961, 34).

Many of us could infer from this observation that we have too much law, and that indeed we are over-regulated. But Freud does not leave the argument with only a description of the neurotic. He concludes that individual longing necessarily remains in conflict with cultural ideals for the preservation of civilization. Certainly we live in a time when law has a much reduced repressive hold on each of us than in the days when Freud wrote. For example, roles and conduct for women and men are much less prescribed; philosophies of childrearing are more accepting and supportive. Even at this, we understand well that reduction in law has not necessarily made for "a return to possibilities of happiness." Passionate longings remain, and we continue to collide not only with cultural ideals, as Freud suggests, but with both descriptive and prescriptive law—gravity and the Ten Commandments.

Our collisions with law and the resulting humiliation and shame we feel are inevitable. Submission to law and its eventual internalization are important not only for survival in our complex cultural context, but for our ability to trust, enabling us to be reciprocally loving and responsive with other human beings. Indeed, without the law, we are adrift in our longings and addicted to fantasies of power and control over others. Psychologically, internalized law represents limit, expectation, and boundary. No boundaries develop without submission and resulting trust.[1]

Law is frightening, and it can easily be abused. We can see in our mind's eye death squads operating in anarchy or secret police under repressive governments executing current "law" with murderous intent. We can recognize deadening legalism in churches where community-dominated correct belief or correct action supplants trusting relationships with one another and with God. Law itself, we are not fooled, is not the source of abundant life. It can be a crushing force that burdens and sickens rather than liberates. Yet law clearly has a place in Jesus' thinking, and we need to understand this fact. What stand does Jesus take on law, and how exactly does it fit into our lives?

Those of us who embrace Jesus' offers of forgiveness and acceptance with joy and relief may find ourselves troubled by his stand on law. Jesus is clear: "Do not think that I have come to abolish the law or the prophets; I have come not to abolish but to fulfill" (Mt 5:17). Introducing a collection of "law sayings" recorded by Matthew in the Sermon on the Mount, Jesus announces, "For truly I tell you, until heaven and earth pass away, not one letter, not one stroke of a letter, will pass from the law until all is accomplished. Therefore, whoever breaks one of the least of these commandments, and teaches others to do the same, will be called least in the kingdom of heaven; but whoever does them and teaches them will be called great in the kingdom of heaven" (Mt 5:18–19). Submission to law is essential. Doing the will of the Father is a foundation to abundant life. Jesus insists that participants in the kingdom must demonstrate their identity by living the law.

Law in Hebrew tradition, we moderns may need to know, is a law by and of an oppressed people, former slaves, who have suffered from unjust law. It is a law based upon consent and peer pressure. It is public, not secret. There are no disappearances with secret trials and executions. King and beggar are equally subject to this law. It is an educational instrument, a guideline for quality living, addressing normal interactions with God and with other human beings. This law is not a method of earning or retaining favor with God. The Israelites to whom Jesus speaks are already a people loved and sustained by God. The law is a gift to the people from God. Obeying the law is an act of thanksgiving, an enactment of their identity, not an attempt to earn acceptance.

Within the New Testament world, at a point in history when Israel's tiny community, occupied by Rome, was threatened with absorption or extinction, adherence to the law, or more specifically to the "holiness code," became associated with honor, purity, and ethnic identity, perhaps even with protection of the community itself from further punishment by God. In the New Testament world, an individual could lose honor for himself and his family by improper social interaction, most particularly by eating with dishonorable people.[2] In this culture it was important to recognize one's enemies, those whose contact might defile oneself and one's family. Marcus Borg addresses this issue:

In response to the threat produced by Roman occupation, the Jewish social world became dominated by the
politics of holiness. . . . Moreover, holiness was understood in a highly specific way, namely as *separation.* To
be holy meant to be separate from everything that would
defile holiness. . . . They were determined to be faithful
to God in order to avoid another outpouring of the divine judgment (1987, 86–87).

Matthew, writing to a Jewish audience, addresses law at
some length by compiling a large collection of Jesus' sayings
on this issue. Where Jesus' introductory statements on law
make clear his adherence to the central significance of law, he
repeatedly confronts legalistic adherence to holiness codes.
Meticulous conformity to law threatens to become a bid for
control—of ourselves, of others, of God. Jesus insists that this
is not righteousness. More specifically, he absolutely resists
any effort to calculate personal righteousness. In the final saying of his introduction, Jesus criticizes two groups revered for
their "righteousness," their careful attention to details of holiness codes: "For I tell you, unless your righteousness exceeds
that of the scribes and Pharisees, you will never enter the
kingdom of heaven" (Mt 5:20). At this point righteousness is
returned to its essential intent, a theme that Jesus elaborates in
the rest of his discourse. As Jesus sees it, the law is an ongoing principle, a guiding force, significant for community, but
never to be accorded the absolute loyalty we offer to God.
The law is given for human well-being, but human beings are
not subordinated to rigid conformity to the law.

Jesus repeatedly confronts the use of law as an indication
of status. In Jesus' parable of the Pharisee and the Toll Collector, the former justifying himself to God in his prayer, and
the latter humbling himself, Jesus concludes: "I tell you, this
man [the tax collector] went down to his home justified rather
than the other; for all who exalt themselves will be humbled,
but all who humble themselves will be exalted" (Lk 18:14).
The final clause is a stinging rebuke not lost on the audience:
the attitude of the toll collector, who would have been hated
for working for the occupying government, indicated that he
more likely lived the law than the Pharisee who "exalted"
himself because of his adherence to the holiness code.

Another characteristic example of Jesus' returning the law to its essential intent is recorded in three of the Gospels: his healing of a man with a withered hand in a synagogue on the Sabbath. Mark records Jesus' challenge, "Is it lawful to do good or to do harm on the Sabbath, to save life or to kill?" (Mk 3:4). New Testament scholar Herman Waetjen, in his *The Origin and Destiny of Humanness,* comments: "Doing good in love has precedence over the rigid observance of this commandment. Human beings were not made for the law, but the law for human beings; and in his interpretation of the Old Testament legislation Jesus lays bare the purpose or goal for which it was intended" (1976, 93). The law itself is not God. Jesus keeps the distinction clear. He heals the man and Matthew records his reminder that righteousness under the law means mercy: "But if you had known what this means, 'I desire mercy, not sacrifice,' you would not have condemned the guiltless. The Son of Man is lord of the Sabbath" (Mt 12:7–8).

In the Sermon on the Mount, Matthew records six sayings on law, frequently called antitheses. Each contains the formula, "You have heard it said . . . but I say unto you . . ." in which Jesus redirects understanding of the law. Jesus asserts: "You have heard that it was said to those of ancient times, 'You shall not murder; and whoever murders shall be liable to judgment.' But I say to you that if you are angry with a brother or a sister, you will be liable to judgment. . . ." (Mt 5:21–22a). At first glance, this appears simply to make the law so difficult that we are convicted of our sinfulness. Herman Waetjen suggests an alternate understanding, based on the significance of the Greek verb, which indicates not feeling angry, but a continual ventilation of anger:

> Clearly then in this first antithesis Jesus upholds the Old Testament law. But he does more: by radicalizing it he draws out its original scope and design. The prohibition of God embraces all kinds of murder, not only physical extermination but also psychological, social and religious forms of human cruelty and destruction (1976, 95).

In other words, one cannot congratulate oneself for refraining from murdering another human being. Rather one should remain self-reflective about harboring intensely angry feelings that could provoke extreme actions proscribed by the law. The attitude of required self-reflection, Waetjen argues, remains throughout the six antitheses. Committing adultery is not so much the issue as is self-reflection on what it means to view members of the opposite sex as objects rather than persons. In a similar vein, Waetjen argues that the cultural practice of using oaths to mark absolute truth telling implies that individuals are ordinarily deceitful. Jesus requires simple truthfulness.

A. E. Harvey, arguing that Jesus' ethical teachings use the wisdom tradition of the ancient world,[3] understands Jesus' method of returning to the essential intent of the law as a jarring, radical departure from the moral presuppositions of his day. Jesus' intent is to persuade or provoke his hearers to understand their relationship to one another differently, rather than to provide a revised set of commandments to be observed. Even Jesus' use of the wisdom tradition is unusual. While most wisdom sayings appeal to common sense and assume a moral view of the universe where virtue is rewarded, Jesus' teachings exceed common sense and offer no guaranteed blessing for virtuous behavior. Instead, he takes contemporary understandings of the law to an extreme, "deliberately [going] far beyond what is reasonable. . . . Again and again we find Jesus using a traditional wisdom formula, but adapting it to convey, not conventional moral axioms, but a disturbing challenge to the presuppositions on which those axioms are based" (Harvey 1990, 143, 155). They not only challenge human wisdom, but they establish an entirely new base of authority: "They could not be commended *merely* as enlightened common sense; they depended on presuppositions that had an authority that was more than human" (ibid., 148). Jesus not only taught these presuppositions, he embodied them. As Harvey notes, "In reality Christ himself was an embodiment of a deeper, hidden wisdom, the 'wisdom of God.' This worked on different presuppositions—such as the infinite extent of the love which God desires us to show to our fellow human beings, regardless of consequences." Both his life and his teachings startle the observer: "It arouses an intensified sense of moral obligation toward God and neighbor" (ibid., 151, 157).

Harvey argues that Jesus' life and teachings assume a kingdom that has already arrived. Inherent in his sayings on law lies a startling invitation to act "*as if* the new age were already here" (ibid., 161). This is no make-believe, Harvey insists. Jesus assumes that evidence of the new age is already apparent: the blind see, the lame walk, and outcasts, such as Zacchaeus, are returned to community.

Jesus, returning the law to its fundamental intent, teaches an enacted redemptive love that promotes quality living not only for the community, but for all people. Truly, the people of God become a blessing to the world. The law Jesus describes jars us awake to hope and love.

We see Jesus approaching the law in three ways: first, he strongly affirms the importance of law. Not a stroke of a letter will be dismissed as irrelevant. Second, he insists that the law serves humankind. Ultimate loyalty is not rendered to the law; human beings do not serve the law. Third, he radicalizes enactment of the law into redemptive love. He alters the essential presuppositions on which the law is founded.

It is precisely these three approaches that describe the significance of law in human personality. Law as an instrument for coming to terms with limits and expectations is essential for human development and human community. Yet law held as an ultimate value and demanding absolute loyalty destroys community and inhibits justice. Lastly, Jesus envisions enacted law as being responsible for ushering in the kingdom of God. Enacted law, beyond measuring and keeping score, becomes radical, extravagant, redeeming love. This final step, jolting us beyond reasonable presuppositions, moves us away from desire to control and into a risky trust and emulation of a loving God.

When we consider Jesus' insistence on the importance of the law in a psychological sense, we approach law as limit, expectation, and boundary. Law, descriptive and prescriptive, establishes our limits. One does not break the law of gravity for long without breaking oneself, and one does not violate the Ten Commandments for long without destroying relationships, community, love, and trust. Prescriptive law also communicates expectations, teaching us what we need to survive in our culture and in the natural world. Limits and expectations establish boundaries: those limits that constitute what can or cannot be done to us and what we can or cannot do to another. Internalizing law is a psychological necessity, and perhaps this is easiest to see with children.

Necessity of law became obvious to one church school teacher when, in an effort to involve her fifth- and sixth-grade students in Bible stories, she had them enact the parable of The Prodigal Son. Once the role-playing ended with the father extravagantly welcoming his delinquent son back into the family, the teacher asked the children, "Well, what do you think?" Her own twelve-year-old son responded with indignation, "That father was stupid! Doesn't he know that kids need rules?" A year before, this boy, learning disabled and barely able to read, had been placed in a tightly structured program that did not bend in any way to his frustration and tantrums. In the safety of unalterable expectations, he began to learn what is needed in order to survive in our complex society. He rapidly began to gain self-esteem and surrender his earlier attempts to control and manipulate other children and adults. Before enrolling in the special program, his concerned parents and permissive school district had collaborated to excuse him from activities that made him uncomfortable, thereby reinforcing his incompetence. As a result, his terror and rage had escalated, and he had spent much disciplinary time in the principal's office. At the time he made his comments about the father in The Prodigal Son, the boy was an expert on the necessity of law. His new school's rigid expectations about how people should be treated and about what he must learn were saving his life, and he knew it.

Since the 1960s popular psychology has advised parents to show respect for and act out an understanding of a child's need for affection, while at the same time it has understated or eliminated the necessity of law. Parental responsibility, therefore, involves "meeting the child's needs" for food and water, shelter, acceptance, and affection. In theory, providing children with these basic elements would meet all that is needed for full human growth and development. Only recently have therapists who work with children begun to speak of the problems associated with children who are granted too much power during their development. Many of these troubled children receive a great deal of understanding and affection during their early years, but are subjected to very few limits. Ironically, some of them develop patterns of manipulation that limit their ability to trust or respond to the love they receive. They tend to believe that they have power and control over the adults in their lives, and therefore resist limits.

This control syndrome also appears in situations of extreme family distress or where children have been neglected or abused. Family therapist Salvador Minuchin studied ten families that had produced more than one delinquent child. He found common in these families that the parents had relinquished their "executive function." Sometimes their roles as leaders and administrators of law had been turned over to one of the children, and discipline had become confusing (Minuchin et al. 1967, 10–11, 217–19). It will come as no surprise that the first requirement for repair of these families is restoring the parental executive function. Therapists help parents assume firm and consistent leadership. Repair also requires wresting leadership control from the hands of children who have seen themselves as little parents with authority over younger siblings.

Similar stories occur in many situations where people work with children from distressed families. City recreation workers, for example, describe rules at their centers as unbendingly rigid. The staff members generally work together to reinforce expectations about the children's treatment of each other, the physical facilities, and the adults. Whenever possible, there are no exceptions to rules of basic decency. One recreation center director from Oakland affirmed, "If we were not strict, the kids would think we didn't care. They need to feel safe. This way, if there is a crisis, the kids will work with us."

Psychiatrist Foster Cline and his colleagues train foster families to care for severely abused and neglected children. Although the families are chosen for their ability to provide warmth and caring, many foster children develop a superficial independence that prevents them from relinquishing control and receiving love. As long as this defense mechanism remains in place, they are not only incapable of reciprocal response, but they are manipulative with adults and cruel to smaller children or animals. Cline and his colleagues, "attachment therapists," train the families to force a child back into the helplessness and hopelessness of infancy. Michael Orlans describes the process:

> The child will seek control; the therapist must set tight limits, leading to control battles . . . [the child] becomes angry and then enraged and expresses his rage to the therapist. He finds this rage neither destroys him nor the

therapist. The therapist remains loving and tolerant throughout.[4]

After therapy, the child will be able to submit to adult authority, form a bond with the parents, and give and receive love. Orlans, Cline, and their colleagues suggest that "spoiled children" as well are insufficiently bonded because of too much gratification of their whims. Without "law" and the acceptance of limits, sufficient bonding falters, they argue, and love cannot be received.

While it is easiest to recognize in children patterns of control syndrome by examining extreme situations, children's tendency to feel magically responsible for controlling their parents—"protecting," they sometimes call it—is relatively common. Elinor Griffin, one of the pioneers of early childhood education, describes "Agatha," an only child, as an example of a child who employed a variety of manipulative maneuvers to prevent her parents from arguing. When she took her behavior at home out of the house and attempted to control relationships at school, her teacher became involved and contacted her parents. Teachers and parents worked together to help Agatha face her limitations and relinquish her desire to control (1982, 121–23). We examine this process further when we explore normal child development in chapter 3.

If an individual's insufficient acceptance of limits leads to disrupted relationships, what happens when an individual lives comfortably within life-enhancing law? A few years ago when a colleague came to our church's family camp with her three-year-old daughter, Patricia, I had an opportunity to observe an excellent example of the answer to my question. Over the week we were quite taken by this self-possessed, unobtrusive child. By the end of the week Patricia had made many friends and knew everyone at her end of the campground by name, totaling about forty people. Knowing that the family was planning to have another child, I teased my colleague that the next time she might have a real child and be unprepared for reality. She replied graciously that she and her husband really loved their little girl. Eighteen months later we had dinner in their home when their second daughter was seven months old. The crawling baby ventured onto a forbidden carpet, and her father interrupted his conversation with us, and said sharply, "Margaret, no." The baby burst into tears, and he picked her up, cuddling her in his lap. Patricia, now four-and-a-half, also climbed into his lap and was welcomed. Their father apologized, "It may seem cruel, but we feel it is important for the children to understand 'no.'" For Margaret and Patricia, potential boundaries were clear and firm and they were not associated with rejection. With due credit to Patricia's genetic characteristics, we gained new understanding of parental contribution to her remarkable capacity to be reciprocal with children and adults alike.

Jesus' first assumption, that the law is essential, is in keeping with a psychological understanding of human development. In order to develop boundaries that enhance reciprocal exchange of love and friendship, human beings must recognize and yield to limitations and expectations. But Jesus does not stop his consideration of law with appropriate responses to human limits and cultural expectations. Jesus' vision of the law "fulfilled" ushers in enactment of the kingdom of God, not the establishment of a small community where nearly everyone merely acknowledges, agrees upon, and enforces the same values. Such enshrining of law in the form of values becomes an idolatry, and law itself threatens to become a method of seeking control, a bid for ultimate safety, which will destroy community. The common temptation runs something like this: "If we all agree and everyone does it our way, we will be safe. Life will no longer be uncertain." In such a situation, human beings must serve the law rather than the law serving human beings. This promotes a politic of holiness rather than a politic of compassion. Such a bid for security through absolutized law represents that instrument of oppression we recognized earlier. At its very worst, it is a law of death squads; at its best it is stifling and boring.

Meticulous adherence to law in our drive for ultimate safety and control, Jesus insists, is not righteousness. Jesus confronts "experts" on the law, the scribes and the Pharisees, with anger: "You brood of vipers! How can you speak good things, when you are evil?" (Mt 12:34). He admonishes his followers, "Unless your righteousness exceeds that of the scribes and Pharisees, you will never enter the Kingdom of heaven" (Mt

5:20). We have been liberated by the law when limit and expectation free us from the frightening power fantasies that are characteristic of childhood and not uncommon for adults. With these boundaries in place, we can enrich our lives through reciprocal loving. However, Jesus does not intend for us to embrace yet another system of imagined control by barricading ourselves into self-righteous communities, away from others and away from a healthy, loving relationship with God. Reminding his hearers that God desires "mercy and not sacrifice," Jesus summarizes the law as radical love: "'You shall love the Lord your God with all your heart, and with all your soul, and with all your mind.' This is the greatest and first commandment. And a second is like it: 'You shall love your neighbor as yourself.' On these two commandments hang all the law and the prophets" (Mt 22:37–40).

But what is this radical love, this righteousness that Jesus contends exceeds that of the scribes and the Pharisees? Harvey argues that Jesus uses the form of the wisdom tradition but takes contemporary understanding of law to an extreme. Jesus presents his own wisdom axioms as disturbing challenges to the very presuppositions of contemporary wisdom. He draws on an authority that is beyond culture and tradition. "But in reality Christ himself was an embodiment of a deeper, hidden wisdom, the 'wisdom of God.' This worked on different presuppositions—such as the infinite extent of the love which God desires us to show to our fellow human beings, regardless of consequences" (Harvey 1990, 151). Jesus jars his hearers into understanding the requirement of the law to be open-hearted, uncalculated giving *as if* the kingdom were already present. It is an invitation to recognize the new era manifested in Jesus' ministry and to become part of it. First, Jesus' rendering of the law confronts us with our limits, the foundation of our finitude with which we live. Second, though we respond to the limits implied by law, we are told that we must not enshrine it. Third, we are challenged to see the law as an invitation to uncalculated generosity, which establishes our position as heirs of the kingdom.

An Answer for Perfectionism

W e have observed Jesus' major concern over the ubiquitous nature of shame and its resulting burden on
human life. Need for forgiveness occupies a central place in
Jesus' system of practical psychology: those alienated through
exclusion because of their unworthiness are invited into forgiveness; those alienated through exclusiveness because of
their merit are confronted with their sinfulness. Jesus, we have
noticed, not only offers forgiveness, but he also affirms the
law. We have understood law in a psychological sense as representing expectation, limitation, and boundary. Law reminds
us that not all things are possible. It brings us face-to-face
with our finitude. But does law, as expectation, also drive us
cruelly to attempt achievement beyond our capabilities? Does
law run wild and frighten us into perfectionism?

I asked a class of graduate students if they felt perfectionism was a problem for our culture at this time in history.
When all concurred, I asked them in what areas of life they
personally felt pressure to achieve perfection. "Well," someone said, "one must of course be a perfect student. Anything
less than an A is failure." "And," said another, "we must certainly be perfect in our careers." "In our private lives," one
woman suggested, "we must be perfectly beautiful, a perfect
spouse, and definitely a perfect parent." "Don't forget being a
perfect homemaker as well," a second woman remarked, "and
let's not forget the new stuff. We must also be perfectly liberated,

perfectly healthy, and perfectly self-actualized." Class members started to laugh. "Yes, of course," the first speaker remarked, "we must be perfectly *not* co-dependent and in the church we must be perfect Christians."

"When you look at this list," I asked, "how do you feel?" The response was a group groan. "Terrible," they agreed.

Perfection has a single, repetitive message: it is not enough to be human, to be limited, to be finite. Global in nature, it is profoundly convincing. No matter how hard we strive for a standard, we never quite measure up. But even when we do achieve, we are not safe.

A woman in her thirties, married with two children, finished her bachelor's degree after persisting for twelve years. Her younger sister wrote on a card, "Sis, you should be proud of yourself. . . . You are a role model for me. I really admire you." Indeed she was a role model, and we all agreed that she had done a wonderful job. She herself expressed relief and joy. But what does it mean to feel proud of yourself? Do we ever experience a smug sense of having arrived? Perhaps Simon Tugwell captures it best when he writes, "Between the trying and the doing there is always a discontinuity; the accomplishment always has the quality of a surprise, a gift, an accident" (1980, 34).

When I had finished my doctorate at Graduate Theological Union in Berkeley, a colleague in my program took me out to lunch. "How does it feel to be finished?" she asked.

"Well," I said thinking it over, "I don't feel any smarter."

Understanding perfectly, she quipped, "Of course not. You could have graduated from Yale or Harvard."

Perfection has an underbelly of panic. Achievement goes dry in our mouths, and we look wistfully at what we did not achieve. And no matter what is achieved in a particular area, new areas emerge to threaten our stability.

This point hit home with me one summer afternoon while walking along the shore of Lake Tahoe in California with a friend from church. My friend glanced at her watch. "Oh, dear," she said, "I have to go back soon. I have a casserole to make for tonight's potluck. I don't know why I didn't get my act together before I left Oakland," she continued crossly scolding herself. "If I had been more organized . . ." She paused a moment reflectively. "I certainly sound like a slave to the kitchen, don't I?"

"Betsy!" I intervened. "You have just criticized yourself from two completely different perspectives: you are trying to be the perfect housewife and the perfect feminist!"

Any standard we meet yields to a standard we have not met, and even when we take to our heart a single standard, we find we never meet it quite well enough. Something strange begins to happen to our striving. Standard itself becomes the goal: good parent becomes perfect parent, good student becomes top student, sincere Christian becomes never-erring saint. Though the standard tends to escalate, we may feel that if we do not meet it, we will consider ourselves unbearable failures. The striving, which originally seemed the stuff of hero journeys,[1] becomes an attempt to earn love, or perhaps avoid rejection. Fleeing the panic of perfectionism, we might find ourselves attempting to arrange life so we are not guilty or so we can judge others. When it slips beyond our consciousness, judgment can become a dangerous form of identity: "Without judgment, I would be nobody." Perhaps we recognize this characteristic in vehement political and religious groups demonizing each other during demonstrations.

Many churches embrace their own particular standard: a doctrine, a code of ethics, a particular behavior, by which members can judge each other as well as outsiders. In other words, the standard eclipses God and requires absolute obedience. The standard becomes an idol, crushing, shaming, and alienating us.

As soon as we possess a new holiness code—be it a form of Christianity, feminism, a system of popular psychology, or political correctness—the good news becomes bad news. An ideology embraced to answer all our life questions is an illusion of safety that will become tyranny, indeed fascism.

Such a system is, of course, also atheism. If, in fact, we have nailed down a perfect code to be followed in detail, we do not need to interact with the God of freedom. Indeed, if we possess a code to which we can cling, we embrace an illusion of safety: we know good and evil; we have become "like God" (Gn 3). Once we have become "like God" within the frightening, wavering safety of our system and our group, we must be entirely good. The only alternative is appalling badness. A perfectionist system leaves us to endure our ubiquitous shame with horror. Shame must be denied and evil must be seen only beyond ourselves and our group.

Conventional wisdom of every age assigns value or honor to individuals or families and in doing so endorses a foundation that can become perfectionism. For culturally accepted reasons, one person, family, or group is valued above another. For example, in the United States today people are valued or honored for physical attractiveness, wealth, education, and competence. These ways of valuing are embraced as avenues to safety; we find the psychology of perfectionism emerging very much as we recognized it above. One is never quite attractive enough, wealthy enough, educated enough, or competent enough. When we accept these conventional standards as measures of our value, we encounter again the underbelly of panic.

In the New Testament world, individuals were valued for their membership in a particular family or clan. As we have already noted in chapters 1 and 2, the culture of Jesus' day was a shame-honor culture based on an expectation of scarcity. In other words, like all commodities, honor was scarce, and any interaction with any person outside one's family or circle of close friends could diminish both personal and family honor. In the case of the Pharisees, a group of lay persons adhering closely to the holiness code could be deemed honorable because of their strict observations of the codes. As we can see from our discussion of law in the last chapter, observation of the holiness codes quickly became a type of perfectionism aimed at finding personal safety, as well as keeping one's family and community safe by buying God's grace through legalistic purity.

Jesus' encounters with adherents to conventional wisdom in the form of holiness codes are confrontational. We noted in chapter 2 that by returning the law to its essential compassionate intent, Jesus advocates an openhanded generosity of spirit that forbids any calculation.

A particularly vivid rendering of Jesus' encounter with legalistic adherence to the holiness codes appears during his dinner at Simon's house (Lk 7:36–50). Simon, the Pharisee, a man of high honor, invited the young rabbi to a formal dinner during which participants reclined at the table. As Joachim Jeremias proposes, the meal may have been in honor of the Sabbath: "We may at all events infer that before the episode which the story relates took place, Jesus had preached a sermon which had impressed them all, the host, the guests, and an uninvited guest, the woman" (1972, 126). Jeremias indicates that the story has to do with the relationship between forgiveness and gratitude. Both Simon and the woman, whom we are told is a "sinner,"[2] are forgiven, but the woman truly grasps the significance of this fact. Her gratitude is extravagant:

> to kiss a person's knee or foot (v. 38) is a sign of the most heartfelt gratitude, such as a man might show to one who had saved his life. How completely the woman was overcome by gratitude towards her savior is shown by the fact that unselfconsciously she took off her head-covering and unbound her hair in order to wipe Jesus' feet, although it was the greatest disgrace for a woman to unbind her hair in the presence of men (ibid.).

Simon, by contrast, continues to trust in his own adherence to the holiness code, the politics of purity (Borg 1987, 86–93). He retains the anxiety associated with conventional wisdom and misses the main point of Jesus' sermon, observing only that Jesus allowed the woman to violate his purity by touching him. Jesus indirectly addresses Simon's concern by offering a parable: two debtors, one greatly in debt and the other slightly in debt, are forgiven by a creditor. Jesus asks his host which debtor would be most grateful. Simon answers correctly, "I suppose the one for whom he canceled the greater debt" (Lk 7:43). Jeremias interprets the parable in the following way:

> The story implies that Jesus in his sermon had offered forgiveness. It is against some such background as this that the parable of the Two Debtors must be understood. In it Jesus replied to Simon's unspoken criticism, and explained why he had allowed a woman who was a sinner to touch him. Why did he allow this to happen?

Thus he points the clear-cut contrast between the great debt and the small, the deep gratitude and the slight. Only the poor can fathom the full meaning of God's goodness. "Do you understand, Simon, that in spite of her sin-burdened life this woman is nearer to God than you?" (1972, 127).

Jesus' confrontation continues beyond Simon's response to the parable. In fact, Luke intends to compare the behavior of the Pharisee as host with the behavior of the woman. Simon's invitation might indicate respect for Jesus as guest of honor, but, we are told, Simon omitted the culturally accepted rituals of hospitality. A rabbi, recognized as a superior, would normally be honored by kisses on his hands or as an equal with kisses on his cheeks; Simon offered no kiss at all. Normal Middle Eastern hospitality would include water to wash one's feet; no water was offered. Hospitality would include anointing an honored guest's head with oil; no anointing was offered. Everyone present would have understood these omissions as a snub. The woman, "a sinner," who gatecrashed this all-male party, provided all the omitted rituals of hospitality. Her tears provided the water to wash his feet, her hair the towel. From her inferior position, she would not dare anoint or kiss his head, but she managed to complete the rituals of hospitality by anointing and kissing his feet.[3]

From his position within conventional wisdom, Simon noticed only that Jesus allowed the woman to violate his purity by allowing her to touch him. Simon's adherence to the holiness code made him both blind and callous. Jesus first uses a parable of two debtors forgiven by a creditor in order to open Simon's eyes to the deeper issues at stake here. Then, in keeping with Jesus' assumption that all human beings need God's forgiveness, he details to his host the obvious failures in hospitality. Kenneth Bailey notes:

There are two kinds of sin and two kinds of sinners, namely Simon and the woman. Simon sins within the law, and the woman outside the law. Sinners like the woman often know that they are sinners; sinners like Simon often do not. Thus repentance comes hardest for the "righteous" (1980, 21).

Perfectionism, or the politics of purity, of any era adheres tightly to conventional wisdom, weighing and measuring value by cultural standards. We have seen in our examination of perfectionism that such adherence is an anxious business. It not only keeps devotees questionably safe and always fearful, but it prevents us from grasping fully the enormous generosity of the gospel. Marcus Borg observes, "whereas first-century Judaism spoke primarily of the holiness of God, Jesus spoke of the compassion of God" (1987, 130). The illusion that we can control our own purity blinds us; thus, we are unable to recognize the extravagant graciousness of God.

How does this perfectionistic human impulse happen? Is this tendency in the human spirit to adhere to conventional wisdom an example of demands imposed on us from childhood having become fixed and expanded in our psyches? Is this impulse a result of faulty role modeling or a combination of bad messages conveyed to us by parents or society? The longing and anxiety we observe in perfectionistic striving is built into human development and is essentially a painful human longing to be completely safe.

For decades clinical psychologists and counselors have observed that clients in therapy "regress"; that is, they become like small children. They re-experience childhood dependency, revisiting terrors of abandonment and the hopelessness and helplessness of infancy.[4] Clinicians have long understood this regression as an essential part of the therapeutic process. In the safety of a therapeutic relationship, normally functioning adults relinquish their usual defenses and explore forgotten suffering that may well control their adult choices from an unconscious level. Clinicians observe that this suffering, when it remains unconscious, drives individuals to repeat hurtful behavior toward themselves and others without much ability to learn from experience. From their knowledge of adults observed in therapy, clinicians have pieced together theories of psychological development including the idea that childhood occurrences strongly affect adult life. In an effort to more fully understand the human suffering they observed, these practitioners joined forces with researchers in child development. From their combined efforts, they concluded that mental illnesses represent lags in normal psychological development.[5] For example, practitioners and researchers concluded that adults who suffer from extreme psychological distress like autism were functioning with the psychology of neonates.[6] Others who experience a panicky need to control combined with a fear of abandonment operate from the psychology of toddlers. With continuing research, the theory has been modified slightly to include the possibility of biological and genetic components in mental illness.

Margaret S. Mahler and her colleagues Fred Pine and Anni Bergman have contributed a major developmental theory that is used widely in therapeutic circles. This research team from the Masters Children's Center in New York suggests that human beings experience psychological birth much as they do biological birth. To put this theory in perspective, they describe the adult psyche as follows:

> For the more or less normal adult, the experience of himself as both fully "in," and fully separate from, the "world out there" is taken for granted as a given of life. Consciousness of self and absorption without awareness of self are two polarities between which he moves with varying degrees of alternation or simultaneity. But this, too, is the result of a slowly unfolding process (1975, 3).

They understand the process of psychological birth as one of separation-individuation.[7] That is, human beings gradually establish a sense of themselves as separate from the world and from other people. They understand the major portion of this process as occurring between the fourth and thirty-sixth month of life, though they caution:

> [The process] is never finished; it remains always active; new phases of the life cycle see new derivatives of the earliest processes still at work (ibid.).

Mahler and her team studied both normal and psychologically troubled infants interacting with their mothers and observed a play between symbiotic attachment and separating or individuation. Beginning their observations with infants four months of age, they suggested that neonates move from "normal autism" into a symbiotic attachment to their mothers. This attachment represents the infant's merging with mother, a delusional unity that offers safety and a sense of omnipotence. At four months the infants were first beginning to separate physically and psychologically from symbiotic union. Mahler describes the psychological process involved in "hatching":

> This is a change of degree rather than of kind, for during the symbiotic stage the child has certainly been highly attentive to the mothering figure. But gradually that attention is combined with a growing store of memories of mother's comings and goings, of "good" and "bad" experiences; the latter were altogether unrelievable by the self, but could be "confidently expected" to be relieved by mother's ministrations (ibid., 54).

In symbiosis infants mold their bodies into the bodies of their mothers, but in hatching they begin to move away. This is represented with the straightening of their bodies away from their mothers. Gradually, of course, as development continues, infants begin to venture off the lap. Mahler describes this new phase as "practicing":

> The early practicing phase, ushered in by the infant's earliest ability to move away physically from mother by crawling, paddling, climbing, and righting himself—yet still holding on: and (2) the practicing period proper . . . characterized by free, upright locomotion (ibid., 65).

The practicing phase ushers in a period of remarkable self-confidence seemingly impervious to pain and stress. Judith Viorst catches the spirit of Mahler's discoveries:

> Stage two, at nine or so months, is an audacious practicing time when we start to physically crawl away from our mother, continuing, however, to return to her as a bountiful home base from which we obtain "emotional refueling." . . . We turn into flaming narcissists. And megalomaniacs. Imperial. The masters of all we survey.

The view from the top of two moving legs has seduced us into a love affair with the world. It, and we, are wonderful (Viorst 1986, 37).

The "practicing" toddler is a bold adventurer. Selma Fraiberg, writing to console parents attempting to cope with children in their first six years, described a little girl "subduing" a tea cart.

She could climb on to the lower shelf of the cart, but the cart perversely moved when she did. After days of futile trials, she finally learned to tackle the tea cart from the back which rested on wooden gliders instead of from the front which rested on wheels. Now she was on it. But how to get out? It was too large a drop to climb out of the cart and her pride was hurt if she was helped out of the cart. She usually fell on her face through any of her own methods of debarkation. But several times a day she set out for the cart, solemn and determined. As she started to climb on to the lower shelf she whimpered very softly, already anticipating, we felt, the danger of getting out and the inevitable fall on her face. . . . She *had* to do it. And finally . . . she discovered a technique for backing out of the cart, reversing the getting-in method. When she achieved this, she crowed with delight and then for days practiced . . . until she had mastered it expertly (1959, 57).

The narcissistic toddler at this stage, so joyful, so confident, and so impervious to injury, captured the imagination of the human potential movement adherents of the 1970s. The movement's proponents envisioned this child as the "natural" state for human beings, whose spontaneity was later spoiled by abusive or clumsy parenting and societal pressures. While we can understand the enthusiasm inspired by the practicing child, these theories were based more on wishful thinking that on scientific observation. The supreme confidence of the narcissistic child is based on the illusion that she is one being with an all-powerful, magical mother. The illusion of union— "hallucinatory or delusional somatopsychic omnipotent fusion

with the . . . mother" (Mahler, Pine, and Bergman 1975, 45)—
which began with symbiosis at about two months, remains in
some form until about eighteen months. At that point, the illusion begins to fracture. Mahler describes this process as it approaches crisis:

> Around 18 months our toddlers seemed quite eager to
> exercise their rapidly growing autonomy to the hilt.
> Increasingly, they chose not to be reminded that at times
> they could not manage on their own. Conflicts ensued
> that seemed to hinge upon the desire to be separate,
> grand, and omnipotent, on the one hand, and to have
> mother magically fulfill their wishes, without their having
> to recognize that help was actually coming from outside,
> on the other. . . It was a characteristic of children of this
> age to use mother as an *extension of the self*—a process
> in which they somehow denied the painful awareness of
> separateness (ibid., 95).

Between eighteen months and three years, gradual matura-
tion of the young child's brain introduces him to the inescapable fact that he is a separate human being, that mother
has a life and interests of her own. Mahler describes this
phase as "rapprochement":

> He now becomes more and more aware, and makes
> greater and greater use, of his physical separateness.
> However, side by side with the growth of his cognitive
> faculties and the increasing differentiation of his emotional
> life, there is also a noticeable waning of his previous im-
> perviousness to frustrations, as well as a diminution of
> what has been a relative obliviousness to his mother's
> presence. Increased separation anxiety can be observed
> (ibid., 76).

Somewhere in the emotionally stormy period we have
called the "terrible twos," each of us learns a frightening truth.
We are not one being with a magical omnipotent mother; we
are small frightened denizens in a big universe. If we were to
describe this awareness in theological terms, we might say

that it is at this point we first experience the reality of our finitude. Theologian Paul Tillich addresses this dilemma: "To be finite is to be insecure" (1967, 195).

The rapprochement transition was demonstrated for me when a couple arrived for marriage counseling accompanied by their three-year-old son, Jerry, their baby-sitting arrangement having failed at the last minute. Experienced parents, they brought a bag full of toys hoping to hold his attention while we worked. As the family was leaving their house, Jerry had grabbed a large wad of play dough; his mother quickly picked up a sheet of plastic. In my office the play dough remained Jerry's toy of choice. He engaged his mother in a game. He tried to put the play dough on my rug, and she slipped the plastic under it. He moved the play dough to the edge of the plastic, and Mom moved the plastic to ensure its place under the dough. Each time, his mother said, "Not on the rug, Jerry. On the plastic." On the third or fourth attempt, she removed the play dough from her son, wrapped it in the plastic, and put it in the bag. Jerry lay on the floor and wailed.

To the casual observer it might appear that Jerry had his heart set on putting the play dough on the rug, but truly the stakes were much higher. Jerry was learning the terrible lesson of rapprochement: Mother had a life of her own. Her priorities were not his; he was not in perfect control. The human fantasy of paradise, so charmingly apparent in the narcissistic infant, shatters as we come face-to-face with the finite creature that we are.

Viorst captures the dilemma:

At eighteen or so months of age, however, our mind gains the capacity to grasp the implications of our separateness. It is then that we see what we are: a small and vulnerable and helpless one-and-a-half-year-old. It is then that we are confronted with the price we have to pay for standing alone. . . .

Lost is the sense of perfection and power that comes from the illusion of being the king of the world, the star of the show.

Lost is the sense of security that derives from the illusion that a child always has a safety net for a mother (1986, 38).

Realization of separateness is not the only hard lesson of rapprochement. The narcissistic infant encased in impervious self-confidence has a simple system of ethics. If she gets what she wants, that is good; and if she does not, that is bad. A mother can find herself transformed in a fraction of a second from the role of good fairy, bestower of all good gifts, into that of wicked witch, tormentor of the helpless. This was demonstrated one day during lunch with a friend. Marie was holding her eleven-month-old son Sam while feeding him an apple. Sam was greatly enjoying the fruit, dribbling the juice down his mother's hand and grinning at me between chews. After ten minutes or so, Marie said, "That's enough." She put him down, put the apple away, and wiped her hand. When she again picked Sam up, he bit her. Good mother transformed into wicked witch was justly punished.

In a few more months, Sam's experience of rage over the disappearing apple will become much more complicated. As the narcissistic child enters rapprochement, his own righteous rage will terrify him. He will know that the person who angers him is not only "bad mom" or "wicked witch," but also the same mother whom he loves and on whom he depends. He is not yet mature enough to know that his intense feelings, so frightening to him, do not in themselves cause harm.

Viorst summarizes:

> In our immature state we cannot hold in our head the strange notion that those who are good can sometimes also be bad. And so our inner images—of mother and of self—are split in two:
>
> There is an all-good self—I'm a totally wonderful person.
>
> And an all-bad self—I'm a totally rotten person.
>
> There is an all-good mother—she gives me everything I need.
>
> And an all-bad mother—she gives me nothing I need . . .
>
> But gradually we learn—if there is love and trust enough—to live with ambivalence. Gradually we learn to mend the split (1986, 42).

As Viorst suggests, Mahler's team is by no means pessimistic about the outcome of rapprochement. The child urged away from Mother by his developing skills returns to her for "refueling." Mahler posits that when the mother is emotionally available to these returns, the child eventually completes individuation, the separating process. He leaves the infant fantasy of paradise and learns, however regretfully, to live with ambivalence. But Mahler has reminded us the process "is never finished," that changes in the life cycle vivify the primitive processes we once thought completed.

Paul Tillich takes Mahler's observation to another level when he proposes, "Finitude in awareness is anxiety" (1967, 191). The maturing human brain introduces us painfully and anxiously to our limits: we are not completely wonderful and we are not completely safe. In other words, we are unequivocally finite. The real danger occurs when the reality of our finitude remains unconscious.

Ernest Becker addresses our terror of finitude by saying that "the idea of death, the fear of it, haunts the human animal like nothing else; it is a mainspring of human activity—activity designed to avoid the fatality of death, to overcome it by denying in some way that it is the final destiny for man" (1973, ix). The human animal, Becker proposes, bears a burden of knowledge that no other animal must bear: we are aware of the fact that we die.

Death is the great insult to human significance, and not only death but finitude itself represents a lingering terror. Terrible things happen, and we cannot stop them. Terrible things happen not just to us, but to those we love. But how does this relate to the rapprochement crisis and repeating occurrences of problems with individuation? Rapprochement introduces each human being to the knowledge of death; and then for the rest of our lives we struggle with that meaning. Is a child's rapprochement anxiety, therefore, a product of bad parenting? Becker is closer to the truth:

> Reality and fear go together naturally. As the human infant is in an even more exposed and helpless situation, it is foolish to assume that the fear response of animals would have disappeared in such a weak and highly sensitive species. It is more reasonable to think that it was instead heightened, as some of the early Darwinians thought: early men who were most afraid were those

who were most realistic about their situation in nature, and they passed on to their offspring a realism that had a high survival value. The result was the emergence of man as we know him: a hyper-anxious animal who constantly invents reasons for anxiety even where there are none (ibid., 17).

Speaking directly to parents who embraced the post–World War II hope for raising perfectly secure children, Becker writes, "If the child has had a very favorable upbringing, it only serves all the better to hide the fear of death" (ibid., 23).

So what is this that we are seeing in the painful system of perfectionism? I suggest that perfectionism is a continual temptation and profoundly human. Perfectionistic striving represents a desperate effort to avoid coming face-to-face with our vulnerability, a frantic scramble to be more than finite. It is a rash attempt to be somehow in control, to quiet the innate gnawing fear founded in our clandestine knowledge of vulnerability and death. If only I am perfect, the logic goes, perfectly friendly, perfectly scholarly, perfectly mothering, perfectly Christian . . . if only I am perfect, perhaps . . . The accusing inner voice is always the same and always hypnotically convincing beyond any reasoning. It drives us with a subdued panic. What you *are* is not enough. It is not sufficient to be human, to be finite, to be vulnerable. You must have a perfect system: a perfect faith system, a perfect psychological system, a perfect weapons system, and then you will be safe . . . maybe. But our perfectionism is a balance beam crossing an abyss. We dare not miss a step. Therefore, we find ourselves living again in the split described by Judith Viorst: Either I am wonderful or I am nothing. Either I am loved by everyone, or I am abandoned. Either every project I undertake is successful or I am a total failure. In perfectionism, narcissism has disguised itself as confidence, and we diligently seek the paradise we lost in rapprochement, the place where we will always be in control and always be safe.

If from the depths of our vulnerability, we cry out to achieve godhead, we serve God who from the depths of compassion chose to be human. Our temptations, as Johannes Metz describes, are understood by Jesus because of his own engagement with universal human temptation:

[The temptations] represent an assault on the radical un-compromising step [Jesus] has taken: to come down from God and become man.

To become man means to become "poor," to have nothing which one might brag about before God. To be-come man means to have no support and no power, save the enthusiasm and commitment of one's own heart (1968, 14).

Metz elaborates the temptation scenario:

"You're hungry," [Satan] tells Jesus. "You need be hungry no longer. You can change all that with a miracle. You stand trembling on a pinnacle, overlooking a dark abyss. You need no longer put up with the frightening experi-ence, this dangerous plight. . . ." Satan's temptation calls upon Jesus to remain strong like God, to stand within a protecting circle of angels, to hang onto his divinity (Philippians 2:6). He urges Jesus not to plunge into the loneliness and futility that is a real part of human exis-tence. . . .

Thus the temptation in the desert would have Jesus betray humanity in the name of God (or, diabolically, God in the name of humanity). Jesus' "no" to Satan is his "yes" to our poverty. He did not cling to his divinity. . . . Instead, Jesus subjected himself to our plight. . . .

He professed and accepted our humanity, he took on and endured our lot, he stepped down from his divinity. He came to us where we really are—with all our broken dreams and lost hopes, with the meaning of existence slipping through our fingers. He came and stood with us, struggling with his whole heart to have us say "yes" to our own innate poverty.

God's fidelity to man is what gives man the courage to be true to himself (ibid., 16, 17, 19).

Perfectionism is our desperate protest against finitude, the toddler in us facing a rapprochement crisis. In the midst of this devastating confrontation with our creaturely vulnerabil-ity, we are invited into radical monotheism. We who would exhaust ourselves trying to be God meet God who has chosen the poverty and powerlessness of being human. Our accept-ability is no longer based upon perfectionism, no longer cen-tered in something we try to control. Rather we are called into the deep tenderness of God's love for us. In the safety of that love, Jesus insists that we will not die of pain and embarrass-ment as we gradually discover the foolishness and manipula-tions of our true selves.

The Holiness of Being Human

F rom the beginning, Scripture suggests there is something
of God in every human being. "So God created humankind in his image," writes the poet in Genesis, "In the
image of God he created them; male and female he created
them" (Gn 1:27). Somehow we carry in us the image of God,
and nothing can remove that fact. Through this image we belong uniquely to God and to all creation. Later in Scripture,
through Jesus of Nazareth, the Incarnation, God made sacred
all human life. Indeed this holiness of being human from
Adam to Jesus to the present represents fulfilling a divine calling to be fully human.

We celebrate these events Sunday by Sunday in Gospel and
liturgy, song and Scripture. But what do they mean? Certainly
there has been no consensus among theologians about the
meaning of the metaphor "image of God." And while we may
celebrate the holiness of Jesus, we may neglect his humanness.
How can we hold together humanness and holiness? And does
the combination say anything about practical psychology?

Without question we brainy bipeds at the top of the food
chain, whether we like it or not, occupy a definitive role. But
the role can express itself in both good and evil. We are
clever and we are dangerous; we are creative and we are destructive; we love and we murder. How can we understand
our unusual status with its gifts and liabilities? Can we, in the
midst of this ambiguity, identify a value in humanness to

match scriptural understandings? Theologians and philosophers over the centuries have tried to identify that which makes human beings unique. Psychologists in the last fifty years have also tried their hands at constructing a theory to recognize the value of human beings.

As we have seen in chapter 3, our significance in biblical tradition does not rest on usual standards of merit: it depends neither on our achievements nor on our adherence to standards of conventional wisdom of any culture in any age. Instead, our perfectionist striving, noble and heroic as it may be, burdens and exhausts us. It more often threatens to become an idolatry rather than a path to holiness. Perfectionism directs us into panicky controlling instead of reverent worship. The image of God in us, our "holiness," lies within the humble limitations of our finitude as did the Incarnation. For those of us who work closely with human beings in their struggle with finitude, the image of God is sometimes strikingly apparent.

On an ordinary Wednesday afternoon at my counseling office, the young man scheduled at two o'clock is a violinist in a San Francisco Bay Area symphony orchestra. Long committed to a loving partnership and to his developing career, he is equally committed to a personal relationship with God. But the world is getting to him: the terrible Oakland-Berkeley firestorm happened just six weeks earlier, and friends and acquaintances are dying of AIDS. He worries about "the kids," local high school students, who seem oblivious to potential dangers in city living. But the significant event came when he went to a nursing home Thanksgiving Day to play for a former colleague, a pianist, who was dying of a degenerative brain disease following a stroke. "Peggy!" he exclaims, beginning to cry, "When I was playing for her, I just knew she was going to die. And she went into a coma the next day, and died four days later." He is overcome and pauses in his story. "Do you know that her own son isn't even coming to her memorial service?" For this son from a close-knit Italian family, such disrespect for kinship ties is appalling. "How can people do things like that?" We talk about God's suffering over the world's pain, of Jesus' wanting to gather Jerusalem to him like a mother hen. I am moved by this talented, vital young man who wonders about his mental balance in a "don't-worry-be-happy" materialistic culture because he feels the suffering of others. I watch him embrace the divine calling to be fully human with its painful empathy.

At three o'clock a retired man arrives. Two years ago he was pushed out of his job in publishing by a new manager who has also since been fired. That painful time we worked through together; now I see him less regularly. He has tried his hand at a variety of small sales jobs that have offended his ethics. At the moment he awaits word about a state job he feels he will enjoy. But his life is much more than work. He maintains several lifelong friendships and belongs to a house-church religious community that he helped found. Having recently discovered a learning disability that affects his attentiveness, he explores it at a community college. He has taken up meditation, and reports what his wife has told him for years: "I'm a worry wart," he tells me with a broad grin. Like the violinist mentioned earlier, he feels burdened by the world's pain, and has begun volunteering for our local congressman. I comment that he has a rich life. Although his life has been hard, with early years marked by poverty and deprivation, at sixty-seven he is enjoying remembering, thinking about what his life has meant. He tells me of a recent men's retreat where someone asked him his long-range plans. His long-range plan is simple: "I want to die with gratitude and grace." He smiles. I am touched by his courage.

At four o'clock an art teacher from an elementary school arrives. She has been in her job only two years despite being in her early forties. She only recently sought credentialing after working in an art supply store for some time. A severe learning disability has made passing the requirements for a California teaching credential hard. She lives with a lingering terror that someone will discover her disability, that she will be disgraced and shamed. The fear isolates her. A product of Catholic schools herself, her standards for student behavior, especially their treatment of each other, are stringent. She is clearly devoted to teaching, and she loves children. Her descriptions of them contain a twinkling warmth. I delight in her demanding love.

Such counseling experiences recall the scriptural metaphor of human value, the image of God. We are human and we are holy. Psychology, as well as biblical theology, has sought to affirm and define human value. Post–World War II humanistic psychology posits an understanding of human beings as inherently precious and possessing practically unlimited potential. Ideas from these theories widely influence contemporary culture. What is this field of psychology, and are its adherents affirming a similar reality as the Christian understanding of human holiness in the biblical tradition?

Humanistic psychology of the post–World War II era has its roots in the work of theorist-practitioner Carl Rogers (1951). Critical of Freud's theory that human beings are primarily motivated by unconscious biological drives and critical of the resulting pessimism in the psychoanalytic school, Rogers began a "client-centered" approach to therapy, arguing that with appropriate empathy and "unconditional positive regard" (Hall and Lindzey 1978, 289), troubled people could blossom into full "self-actualization," a term he borrowed from Kurt Goldstein, who understood "self-actualization" or "self-realization" as the master motive for human growth (ibid., 249). Abraham Maslow also adopted Rogers's optimism and Goldstein's term, "self-actualization." The term as used by Rogers and Maslow posited nearly unlimited potential for human growth and development and became enormously popular. However, a significant feature of Goldstein's theory was lost: the need to "come to terms" with one's environment (ibid.).

Maslow, speculating about psychological health, argued that much psychological theory had been developed from work with troubled people, and, therefore, offered an incomplete understanding of human development and potential. He undertook a study of psychologically healthy people (1968). Interviewing colleagues and public figures like Eleanor Roosevelt and examining biographies of such luminaries as Abraham Lincoln and Walt Whitman, Maslow produced a description of the self-actualized adult, the vigorously healthy, content, and productive individual (ibid., 26).[1]

From this social scientific description of the characteristics he observed in outstanding individual lives, Maslow proceeded to speculate about the type of environment that is likely to produce such people. He described a "hierarchy of needs" that if met, he proposed, would enable a person to arrive at vigorous and creative psychological health. It was, he suggested, the nature of human beings to develop into fully healthy, self-actualized adults, provided that their needs for physiological survival, safety, belonging, esteem, and cognitive and aesthetic development were met. In this framework, Maslow retained Goldstein's original sense of self-actualization as a primary motivating force in human beings, but abandoned Goldstein's view that self-actualization required the individual to "come to terms" with his or her environment (Hall and Lindzey 1978, 250–51). As a consequence, self-actualization in Maslow's framework became a birthright and an obligation to parents and society to see that the needs of the next generation were met.[2]

Maslow's philosophy gained in popularity and influence partly because it moved in harmony with the postwar American enthusiasm for children. Americans returned from World War II interested in hearth and family and in protecting the childhood of their offspring for whom they had fought. Benjamin Spock's best seller, *Baby and Child Care,* which advocated a loosening of rigid scheduling for children and provided practical tips for firm but gentle guidance, was first published in 1945. Clinicians and theorists, recognizing the truth in Freud's assertion that the "child is father of the man," wrote with great enthusiasm about the value of human beings and the possibilities for raising children free of the hatred and envy that cause war. Correct handling of children became the answer to future world problems, and psychologists, including Maslow, raised questions about the types of childhood that produce unusual lives. Erik Erikson's study of Gandhi (1969), for example, arose from the spirit of these inquiries. With the guidance of psychologists, parents set out to prepare their children, the baby boomer generation, to create a better world. Reflecting this optimism and expectation, *Time* magazine designated the boomer generation as its Man of the Year in 1967. In his book chronicling the baby boomer generation, which he designates as those people born between 1946 and 1964, Landon Jones writes:

The editors of *Time* honored the "Under-25 Generation" as its Man of the Year in 1967. "In its lifetime," *Time* wrote, "this promising generation could land on the moon, cure cancer and the common cold, lay out blight-proof, smog-free cities, help end racial prejudice, enrich

the underdeveloped world and, no doubt, write an end
to poverty and war" (1980, 75).

The enthusiasm of Maslow and other humanistic psychologists was taken up by zealous writers of self-help and popular
psychology in the 1960s and 1970s. A proliferation of optimistic literature ensued, advocating fulfilled lives through
communication skills, expression of feelings, taking responsibility for one's own life, dropping out, finding a "meaningful"
career, and reexperiencing childhood trauma. Broadly speaking, the human potential movement promised that human beings, following their own impulses and desires, would evolve
into a new, more humane, and more fulfilled human race, de-
void of warlike inclinations. Correct parenting was needed to
bring this about, but if life had not gone well, individuals
could repair their pasts through therapy and still evolve into
healthy, happy, and fulfilled human beings.

It is difficult to miss the attractiveness of these ideas. Any
church droning away about sin and redemption during these
years found itself empty, congregants having fled to encounter
groups, growth workshops, or therapists. To place all evil in
one's parents and society freed an individual to explore with
enthusiasm and vigor a potential that was theoretically limitless.

Such a philosophy, enormously attractive, was enormously
flawed. In the 1980s it became apparent that enthusiastic
focus on the self and all its potential produced not socially
concerned public servants, disciplined scientists, and diplo-
mats, but rather individuals who were self-centered, isolated,
and sometimes incompetent: "the Me Generation." Moreover,
members of the boomer generation felt burdened by expectations and oppressed by assumptions about their unlimited potential. One woman in the early wave of the baby boomers,
having achieved a doctorate and a university job by age thirty-
two, remarked as she approached forty that she kept thinking
she should have done more with her life: "something wonderful." Developmental psychologist Jerome Kagan observes the
following about a demonstration of parental concern that
began with the boomers:

And a small proportion of American children, whose af-
fluent parents shower them with affection and gifts out

of a desire to create in them feelings of confidence and self-worth, become apathetic, depressed adolescents because they do not believe they deserve such continuous privilege (1984, 241).

Throughout the 1980s the theorists and popularizers alike understood need as something that could be fulfilled, and when fulfilled, would yield a sense of completeness, security, and contentment. It has become increasingly apparent, however, that "getting one's needs met" is an endless and futile process. Phillip Cushman argues that such a philosophy of the human self as an isolated entity is, in fact, empty:

I believe that in the post–World War II era in the United States, there are indications that the *present* configuration of the bounded, masterful self is the empty self. By this I mean that our terrain has shaped a self that experiences a significant absence of community, tradition, and shared meaning. It experiences these social absences and their consequences "interiorly" as a lack of personal conviction and worth, and it embodies the absences as a chronic, undifferentiated emotional hunger. The post–World War II self thus yearns to acquire and consume as an unconscious way of compensating for what has been lost: It is empty (1990).

In response to this emptiness and emotional hunger, some psychologists have turned toward spirituality, often appropriating Eastern religious philosophies to serve a Western concern for individual inner peace and happiness. Unfortunately, the concern continues to center on the isolated individual. Harvey Cox addresses this issue in describing the failings of postwar psychological thought:

Western psychology itself is now floundering badly and many psychologists are eagerly turning to Eastern teaching as a possible means of deliverance. . . . All psychologists today are in part children of the Enlightenment and of its condescending attitude toward superstition and spirituality. They are alienated by the history of their discipline from most of their own Western religious tradition.

. . . Their effort to understand the psyche without reference to the psyche's relationship to other realms of being has resulted in shallowness and aridity (1977, 74–76).

Cox compares Western psychology to Narcissus of the Greek myth, forever staring into his own reflection, frozen and without contact with a broader world.

Understandings of spirituality have reappeared in popular psychology. These include the last book of family therapy pioneer Virginia Satir (1988), as well as contributions from representatives of the Twelve Step programs and lectures of the popularizer John Bradshaw.

Probably the most influential contributor to current popular spirituality is C. G. Jung. A believer in God and developer of one of the major twentieth-century systems for understanding human personality, Jung became fascinated with belief systems and myths that appear in diverse cultures around the world. Part of Jung's system strives to explain human similarity in spite of differences in culture and individual experience through the concept of "collective unconscious":

The collective unconscious is the storehouse of latent memory traces inherited from one's ancestral past, a past that includes not only the racial history of humans as a separate species but their prehuman or animal ancestry as well. The collective unconscious is the psychic residue of human evolutionary development (Hall and Lindzey 1978, 118).

According to Jung, each individual is born with a collective unconscious that he or she shares with the entire human race. Within the collective unconscious are shared thought forms, called archetypes. One such concept or thought form is "Mother," since all human generations share an experience of mother. Another is "evil," and a third, "masculine" and "feminine." Many other archetypes have been suggested, such as the "goddess," the "wise old woman," and the "wizard." In popularized use of Jungian theory, individuals try to become aware of and "listen to" their archetypes. A man may try to develop his feminine side, called "the Anima," or a woman her masculine side, "the Animus." Individuals hope to become aware of many archetypes in their journeys toward personal wholeness and maturity, symbolized by the completion of a "personal mandala," a circular symbol of the universe borrowed from Hinduism or Buddhism representing life's wholeness. For followers of Jung, the mandala represents the development of all aspects of the psyche.

Jung's ideas have been linked to those of Joseph Campbell. Campbell was an English professor, less a systematic thinker than an enthusiastic eclectic, who became fascinated with likenesses he found in mythologies and art around the world. His observations added credibility to Jung's already fascinating concept of the collective unconscious. Campbell, a charming speaker, made popular a lifetime of observations toward the end of his life, speaking to lay audiences and recording an often-aired series on public television. The concept Campbell contributed to popular culture is the idea of the hero journey. He noted that every culture had some form of hero story. He admonished his listeners to "follow your passion." This counsel has generally been understood to mean finding a fulfilling career or life challenge. Unfortunately, it has been taken as a call for people to experience continual bliss.

The enormous popularity of both Jung and Campbell led to interest in world religions and the adoption into popular culture of terms like *archetype, mandala,* and *hero journey*. In contrast with the 1970s when self-actualization was the goal of life, the 1980s emphasized life's goal as continuing one's journey and completing one's personal mandala. The term *spirituality* came to be applied to any profound emotional experiences, particularly those understood as emanating from an archetype or contributing to one's understanding of wisdom obtained from a particular archetype. The understanding of *spiritual* in this complex system remains on the human level, however, and does not imply the existence of a transcendent God, although some have integrated Jung's thought into a framework that includes such a belief.

Does the archetypal hero journey described by Campbell or the goal of completing one's personal mandala implied by Jung represent an understanding of the specialness or holiness of being human similar to that affirmed by the Christian tradition? I propose that the views of Campbell and Jung differ from the Christian concept of human value or holiness.

Since holiness involves accepting a divine calling to be completely human, we need to start with a basic understanding of what it means to be human. Clearly being human includes being born to finite parents as a creature, finite ourselves. And as vulnerable and intelligent creatures, which we considered in chapter 3 when discussing Ernest Becker's work, we live with an awareness of vulnerability and death. As Maslow's hierarchy of needs suggests, we are bodies with physiological needs, safety needs, and social needs that are so definite that we may not survive if those needs are not met. It is apparent that we need food, water, sleep, shelter, and protection, but studies of institutionalized infants have demonstrated that social and affectional needs are so strong from birth that infants who receive insufficient attention and handling die (Spitz 1965, 35–51). It is also clear that human beings who have all their basic needs met seem to become aware of other yearnings. As noted above, Maslow and many like him understood these yearnings or needs as something that could be met and believed that their fulfillment would yield a sense of completeness, security, and contentment. But the needy feeling has a much more basic source. As Becker observed, human beings as creatures are highly intelligent and very vulnerable. At some level, we know that bad things happen to us and to those we love and that we cannot prevent them. At the very base, we know that we die. It is this vulnerability, and the resulting uneasiness, however hidden from ourselves, that remains with us all our lives. Anxiety, therefore, as well as potential, is a normal part of the human condition. Theologian Paul Tillich, as I quoted in chapter 3, writes, "To be finite is to be insecure" (1967, 195). This in itself runs counter to the optimism of popular culture.

If then we are to take basic anxiety seriously as part of the human condition, we must also recognize that no amount of need fulfillment, no heroic accomplishment, nor psychological healing will alleviate it. If we live with this burdensome sense of limit, how then do we understand our holiness?

In the biblical tradition human holiness, that something of God in each of us, is never achieved. Rather, without control on our part, it is given: through creation, God's choosing, the Incarnation, the Cross, and the Resurrection. We are promised complete fulfillment of that holiness in ourselves and in the entire creation in the Jubilee, Christ's second coming. Holiness, irrevocable and the source of immense joy, is granted through the abundant love and graciousness of God, Creator of the Universe. It lies deeply embedded in our limited creatureliness. It is not that we strive heroically to achieve godliness, and God recognizes our merit. Instead, we celebrate a God who chose to become finite and to live fully within the confines of anxiety-ridden finitude all the way to death. This God invites us into received holiness embedded in finitude. Ironically, all true happiness—*blessing,* to use the Christian word—occurs precisely within the scope of our limited creatureliness.

But let us take a look at received holiness in Christian tradition, celebrated in liturgy, readings, and sermons Sunday by Sunday. It begins, of course, with creation. "So God created humankind in his own image; in the image of God he created them, male and female he created them. . . . And God saw everything that he had made, and indeed, it was very good" (Gn 1:27; 31a).

Moreover, the God who created humankind also is in love with us and seeks to have a relationship with us. This courting, this choosing by God, we observe in Psalm 8: "What are human beings that you are mindful of them, mortals that you care for them? Yet you have made them a little lower than God, and crowned them with glory and honor" (Ps 8:4–5). Another psalm celebrates, "I praise you, for I am fearfully and wonderfully made" (Ps 139:14). Human value appears in God's tender seeking of Israel, a people chosen not for their merit but by God's decision, to become "holy" or set apart for God, a servant people chosen to bless the world.

Holiness in human beings has its origin in our being made in the image of God; through creation itself, we are granted holiness. It continues through God's choosing of a people, the Jews, to be a holy servant community. The gift of holiness culminates in God's entrance into finitude through his son Jesus of Nazareth. The Incarnation makes holy all human life. Our very living has become sacred. Perhaps the gift becomes most conscious as we accept God's invitation to enter a loving relationship.

The intent of this relationship, however, is not for us to get our needs met. Ancient Israel, chosen as God's people through love, was not intended as a cosmic pet, but rather as a servant people "by which all nations of the world shall bless themselves." In like manner, God's choosing of us involves an increasing invitation to align ourselves with God's priorities— "the Kingdom of God." Thus, we exercise the godliness inherent in our humanity by becoming separate to God and God's priorities. Indeed, the central human desire to be unique or special, treasured and beloved, rests in this holiness. Through it we are called to a central sense of vocation: concern for others and for the creation. The invitation to separateness is also an invitation to community, the servant community of a chosen people.

Our exercise of holiness and its accompanying sense of blessing involves not so much becoming something better than we are, but rather entering into our finitude with all its vulnerability and terrors. Holiness does not remove us from the limitations of our creatureliness; rather, it is an invitation to live in frank acceptance of our finitude. In this regard, God's choice to enter into finitude in the person of Jesus—the Incarnation—has much to say to us about holiness. The way Jesus lived his life provides us with a concrete way to understand how we are to respond to the invitation to holiness, which I discuss below. But on a more basic level, the Incarnation also reveals God's choice to sanctify all human experience. In a sermon on Christmas, Frederick Buechner captures this insight:

> Those who believe in God can never in a way be sure of him again. Once they have seen him in a stable, they can never be sure where he will appear or to what lengths he will go or to what ludicrous depths of self-humiliation he will descend in his wild pursuit of man. If holiness and the awful power and majesty of God were present in this least auspicious of all events, this birth of a peasant's child, then there is no place or time so lowly and earthbound but that holiness can be present there too (1969, 13).

In passionate pursuit of humanity, God chose to accept and sanctify the limits of human need in all its forms, to experience the life cycle with all its uncertainties, and to accept death. God in Jesus of Nazareth chose powerlessness and vulnerability. We see Jesus in the Gospels struggling to make concrete in his life the commitment he enters into at baptism. We see him experience limits of energy. We see him as unable magically to win all, experiencing limits of persuasiveness. We recognize his suffering in grief for friends, his frustration over Jerusalem, his sense of rejection and abandonment, and his moral and psychological struggle before submitting to arrest, torture, and death. Received holiness abides in the depths of life as it is, finitude in all its terrors.

But clearly, in searching for the holiness of the Incarnation, we can become very uncomfortable with the messiness of daily human life in ourselves and in Jesus. Much better to hold a stained glass version of Jesus' holiness. Many times Christians have been tempted to make Jesus only divine: magically able to know the future, magically able to read people's thoughts, magically able to use God's power as he chooses. Such an understanding of the Incarnation robs it of its power and demeans the holiness of humanity intended for all of us. There is a powerful temptation to view God as a divine safety net who will attend to our every need. In a sense, God becomes an eternal mother replacing "Mother" whom we left at the narcissistic infant period of our lives as we saw in chapter 3. Following this theology, our God safety net will provide all our needs without expecting too much of us. Such a view of God and of the Incarnation has enormous appeal because it promises to address our fear of finitude through a return to the narcissistic fantasy of toddlerhood where we imagined safety and control through our control of mother.

This longing is captured by Judith Viorst in *Necessary Losses:*

"I have always felt," says one of Dr. Smith's patients, "there is a remote person somewhere who would do everything for me, somebody who would fulfill every need in some magical fairylike manner and see to it I would be able to get whatever I want without putting out any effort for it" (1986, 31).

Although it is tempting to distance ourselves from the fantasies of Dr. Smith's patient, I suggest that each of us in the depth of our hearts longs for something to make us unique, special, the only one, and completely safe, or perhaps we long for someone who will always find us wonderful and make the world smooth for us. And these longings for a perfect world, shaped by not-too-conscious interpretations of our experience, do not often make themselves apparent to us. Whatever particular fantasy of safety and specialness we have set our hearts upon, we will generally feel our life depends upon it, and the intensity of our longing makes us dangerous. This longing, in fact, often leads people to try to control and manipulate the object of their desire. In his work with intensely suffering people, Otto Kernberg describes an extreme version:

> There is no real "dependency" in the sense of love for the ideal object [idealized person; therapist] and concern for it. On a deeper level the idealized person is treated ruthlessly, possessively, as an extension of the patient himself. . . . The need to *control* the idealized objects, to use them in attempts to manipulate and exploit the environment and to "destroy potential enemies," is linked with inordinate pride in the "possession" of these perfect objects totally dedicated to the patient. Underneath the feelings of insecurity, self-criticism, and inferiority that patients with borderline personality organization present, one can frequently find grandiose and omnipotent trends. These very often take the form of a strong unconscious conviction that they have the right to expect gratification and homage from others, to be treated as privileged, special persons (1975, 33).

In extreme form, this description basically represents what many of us in the depth of our beings expect from God. Either we pretty much get what we want, or God does not love us. Either our projects succeed, or we are somehow bad Christians. While discussing our inevitable fall from infant narcissism, one student remarked, "We somehow expect God to make good things happen for us, and that indicates God is taking care of our self-esteem." Concepts of "meeting our needs" from Maslovian theory have become embedded in the culture and infiltrate our theology.

If we understand God as a magical safety net, however, crises in faith are inevitable. "If God really loved me, I would be married," I hear often. Or, as others say, "If God cared about me, I would have a job I really love." "What's the point in being a Christian, if God isn't interested in acting on what I see as important?" one frustrated student demanded.

If Jesus' incarnation was not just narcissistic grandiosity with God as the idealized object, a divine safety net that kept anything bad from happening, how can we understand the Incarnation, and what might it say about holiness in human life? Jesus moved through his life with continual openness to received holiness, working out what this commitment meant in practical living. He fulfilled the divine calling to be truly human through loving and grieving, working and feasting, telling truth and suffering consequences. His receptivity to holiness involved a frank acceptance of finitude with all its terrors and limitations. Jesus began his career by submitting to a baptism of repentance. But for what does this man, whom we have understood to be without sin, repent? The stories of Jesus' temptation in the wilderness provide a clue.

Following his baptism, Jesus undertook a forty-day fast and retreat in the wilderness to struggle with the meaning of this commission to which he was called "Son of God" or "New Human Being."[3] In the temptation stories, he demonstrates received holiness and radical acceptance of finitude. Indeed, Jesus demonstrates radical freedom from Maslow's hierarchy of needs: physiological needs, safety needs, belongingness needs, and esteem needs. He is in line with God's power through relationship but refuses to use it in a display of magic to feed himself or others:

> The tempter came to him and said, "If you are the Son of God, command these stones to become loaves of bread." But he answered, "It is written, 'One does not live by bread alone, but by every word that comes from the mouth of God'" (Mt 4:3).

Jesus also refuses to use God's power to meet his esteem needs:

Then the devil took him to the holy city and placed him on the pinnacle of the temple, saying to him, "If you are the Son of God, throw yourself down; for it is written, 'He will command his angels concerning you,' and 'On their hands they will bear you up, so that you will not dash your foot against a stone.'" Jesus said to him, "Again it is written, 'Do not put the Lord your God to the test'" (Mt 4:6).

I believe that Jesus sets aside at his baptism and in the wilderness the powerful human longing to be God knowing good and evil, ultimately safe by means of his own power, in control of the universe, and able to pass judgment on himself and others. His life, as we know it in the Gospels, bears out a full acceptance of the conditions of finitude. He is a radical monotheist[4] submitting to God, trusting God, open to received holiness, but without any design to control the flow of God's power to meet his needs.

It is interesting to note, then, that in the context of embracing his finitude, Jesus resembles Maslow's self-actualized human being. He has a "superior perception of reality," an autonomy that resists enculturation, a "democratic character structure," a problem-centeredness. His life demonstrates acceptance of self and others, spontaneity, detachment and desire for privacy, freshness of appreciation and richness of emotional reaction, "identification with the human species," good interpersonal relations, creativity, and a frequency of "peak experiences" (Maslow's term for what we might understand as experiences of God's presence) (Maslow 1968, 25). There is one notable exception, however: none of these personal attributes are ends in themselves, not results of Jesus' personal striving for growth, but rather the products of received holiness through Jesus' relationship with God. And again Jesus' heroic life is not the result of his enactment of an archetypal hero journey, but a result of living his finitude in received holiness, accepting empowerment by and vocational call from God. Ironically, unless he were able to release the human longing for control and safety against the vulnerability of finitude, he would have been unable to receive the holiness offered him by God. In life, such release of the human passion for control is experienced as a baptism of repentance and death.

Before we conclude, let us briefly explore what this baptism of repentance and death looks like in a clinical setting. Seasoned counselors and therapists have long recognized that people who seek help, and indeed most of us, do not really want to change. Most of us really prefer that the world change to make things more comfortable for us. Most of us harbor a fantasy, the longing for a perfect world or a perfect situation. Without this longing, we often tell ourselves, our lives would have no meaning. We say things like, "If only I could find someone who would really listen to me . . ." "If only I could heal my psychological wounds . . ." "If only I could find someone to be my mother." Or more directly to the therapist, "If only *you* would be my mother." Ironically, as long as a passionately held fantasy persists, the individual will never find a person who listens quite well enough, will never find adequate healing, will never find someone adequate enough to replace the lost mother. It is only through a slow, gentle process that people relinquish their most treasured fantasy, control of holiness on their own terms, and at last are able to receive the holiness of God offered in the midst of vulnerable finitude. Such a letting go always feels devastating, like a terrible death.

A person in therapy—and most of us as we grapple with life—endures a multitude of little deaths, not the least of which is the death of the idea that parents, mentor, and/or therapist are an idealized mother figure always available to bolster self-esteem and meet every need. The baptisms of life are no quick dip in the Jordan, but instead are repeated visions of who we truly are and what fantasies of power we have been spinning. As we come to terms with the impossibility of satisfying our heart's longing, we enter into disappointment, grief, and rage. In other words, we come with passionate reluctance to our encounters with these deaths.

Penny entered into one such baptism more easily than many. She first sought counseling with me after a devastating trip to her parent's home. At twenty-five, this happily married college graduate and mother of two preschool children wanted more than anything in the world for her parents to understand and accept her exactly for herself. The oldest of three—she had two younger brothers—Penny was raised on a hog farm in Iowa close to her paternal grandparents. Born when her mother was fifteen and adopted in infancy by her stepfather, Penny had never met her biological father. Throughout her life, much had been made of the adoption: "Your [adopted] father loves you like his own; he even sent you to college." The truth of the matter, however, was that Penny's father had been a tyrant, belittling all three children for their mistakes, and Penny felt he especially singled her out. Her mother was and continued to be completely submissive, and it was not until Penny went off to college that she discovered other families did not act like hers.

Trouble had been brewing before the trip. A year before, Penny and her husband had moved to California. Penny's parents had worried about her living in a strange new culture so far away from family. Indeed, Penny and James were influenced by eating trends in their new environment and had eliminated red meat from their diet, becoming semi-vegetarians. In addition, Penny's husband, James, a bright young pastor, had begun writing for a demominational magazine. Initially, Penny's father had eagerly anticipated James's first article, but felt humiliated to discover he did not understand it. In short, Penny's parents experienced their daughter's move, her shift in eating habits, and James's complex theology as personal rebuffs against them and their values.

The entire trip was, in fact, a disaster. Due to illness in James's family and complicated travel arrangements, James and Penny arrived a day later than originally planned. Neither one of her parents spoke to her directly for the first twenty-four hours. During the stay, they expected Penny, her husband, and their children to be on the farm at all times. No evening trips into town were planned, and any absence from the farm was considered an offense. Penny's father spent much of the time relating embarrassing memories about her childhood to her children. Her mother continually talked about her brother and sister-in-law who had settled in town. Penny felt rejected and was deeply hurt. At the time of our appointment, she "couldn't" call or write her family and dreaded that they might call her. She wanted to "show them" she was "more than a housewife," and repeatedly asked, "Why can't they accept me for myself?"

As she and I reflected on this conflict, it became increasingly apparent to Penny that she and James lived comfortably in a world entirely foreign to her parents. It was not that they did not respect her; they were baffled by her and felt judged by her. She had rejected values by which they lived. Penny's longing for acceptance died reluctantly. "What is it like for you," I asked, "to realize that they will never be parents who can understand and accept you exactly for who you are?" Penny burst into tears and wept for several minutes. Apparently she cried off and on for most of the week, but at our next appointment there was a difference. She genuinely saw her parents for who they were with many of their limits and failings. She no longer waited for them to affirm her growth and sophistication. The problems were by no means solved, but Penny was better equipped to face reality as it was and handle the problems rather than being repeatedly injured by her unfulfilled longing. She was able to contact her parents by mail and by telephone. Although her father's tirades, while somewhat less frequent, certainly made their appearances, and her mother continued to support him in whatever he did, Penny no longer let her parents' behavior rule her life. She had endured the baptism by surrendering her dearest hope of controlling her parents' attitude toward her and had finally become capable of moving ahead as an independent person. As a result, Penny entered into a fuller life based more firmly on the reality of being a finite woman who is loved and empowered by God. She took another step in the divine vocation of being human.

Our holiness, then, is received and our lives are blessed. We are holy from creation, from election, from the Incarnation, and within community. Our holiness is enriched as we continue to align ourselves with the priorities and blessings of God. Later in this book, I demonstrate how the process is fulfilled in the Cross and Resurrection. Indeed we find ourselves unique, special, and beloved—three longings of the human heart. They are gifts to us, but we do not control them. We belong to God and to one another. In the safety of God's love and blessing, we will continue to have moments of courage in which we identify and release our embarrassing secret designs for power and control. With each painful little death of these inhibiting qualities within ourselves, we become more and more able to live our finitude and to receive the generously offered holiness of God. These moments of awareness reveal to us those places where our grasping hearts interfere with that which God would willingly give. In the words of one pastor: "What we grasped at in the fall is given us in the cross."[5] We are beloved heirs of the Kingdom.

Buechner reflects on this love of God as demonstrated in the Incarnation:

> This [God's power present at the birth of a peasant's child] means that we are never safe, that there is no place where we can hide from God, no place where we are safe from his power to break in two and recreate the human heart because it is just where he seems most helpless that he is most strong, and just where we least expect him that he comes most fully (1969, 13–14).

The Function of Responsibility

W e embody an untarnished holiness, and by God's design nothing we do can change that fact. We are created in the image of God and chosen for friendship with God. We are forgiven for the isolating, perfectionistic burdens we undertake in our futile efforts to become God, to be ultimately safe. The call to friendship is a call to community, a call to love one another and to care for our world. In the biblical tradition, we are a servant people called that the nations of the world might bless themselves.

For most of us as servant people, being loyal to God includes being loyal to this call, caring for others and acting as stewards for our world. The call influences the way in which we execute our jobs and careers. It guides our choices of work and volunteer activities. For most, the call to service and caring contributes purpose to our lives, to the way we live in our families and express neighborliness. Being helpful, however, we find at some points is complicated. A saying from one church's Sunday bulletin captures the dilemma:

> Involvement with people is always a very delicate thing—it requires real maturity to become involved and not get all messed up.[1]

Helping other people is not an easy matter. As helpers we sometimes find that the individual whom we set out to support has become inordinately dependent upon us. The desperate situation has gotten worse. In spite of frequent calls seeking our help and long hours on the phone, our subject remains embroiled in troubles, becoming resentful of us and finally rejecting our suggestions. We are suddenly seen as interfering and condescending meddlers, and indeed we who began by trying "to become involved" find ourselves "all messed up."

Jesus, the New Human Being,[2] who lived within the confines of finitude empowered by God, extended himself to serve others throughout the Gospels. Exploring Jesus' ministry as helper can provide useful insights in determining a model for caring. In Mark 10:46–52, for example, Jesus heals Bartimaeus, a blind beggar seated by the side of the road. The form of the story is an interesting one. When Bartimaeus realizes that Jesus is passing, he cries out to him, and the crowd tries to silence him. But he shouts again, and Jesus acknowledges him. The crowd switches its approach, at this point, and encourages him. Jesus asks that Bartimaeus come to him and then asks what he can do for him. Bartimaeus requests that he receive his sight, and Jesus grants it, but also attributes the healing to Bartimaeus himself: "Your faith has made you well" (Mk 10:52a).

Noticeably lacking in this story is any sense of condescending pity on Jesus' part. The dialogue is adult to adult. Bartimaeus is not approached as a pitiable victim, and he experiences no loss of dignity in the healing. Unlike the crowd, Jesus does not need to ignore Bartimaeus, to deny the desperateness of his situation. He also makes no attempt to rescue the man. Jesus simply asks that Bartimaeus approach him. He recognizes the integrity of Bartimaeus's person and respects it throughout, never assuming he knows best what the man needs. He asks what Bartimaeus wants from him. This form of healing recognizes power within the individual. Jesus acknowledges this in his parting comment: "Your faith has made you well" (Mk 10:52a). The helping itself is empowering rather than demeaning.

We find a similar story in Mark 5:25–34. A woman with "a flow of blood" touches Jesus' robe in hopes of being healed. Jesus, aware of "power" going out of him, calls attention to the incident and invites the woman into a dialogue. She, like Bartimaeus, takes a risk and behaves differently from the expectations of the crowd. Hemorrhaging as she is, it is certainly questionable for her to be in public and illegal, according to laws of purity, for her in such a condition to touch a rabbi. Nevertheless, her determination enables her to respond to her situation. She takes responsibility. Again the dialogue with the woman is adult to adult; there is no condescension. Jesus finds out what happened and acknowledges the power within the woman that enabled her healing. "Daughter, your faith has made you well" (Mk 5:34). Through their "faith"—here demonstrated as a frantic, risk-taking determination—Jesus empowers those he heals.

There are a number of healing stories in the Gospels following this same pattern: determined seeking, resistance of the crowd, renewed seeking, Jesus' response, and an ensuing dialogue, healing, and affirmation of faith. In some of the stories the affirmed faith is that of the supplicant; in other stories from this first-century, strong group-oriented culture, the faith is that of family or friends. In each situation there is one person who demonstrates determination. Matthew records a saying that encapsulates this risk-taking seeking:

Ask and you shall receive. Seek and you shall find.
Knock and it shall be opened to you (Mt 7:7–8).

In these stories we observe at least one person who asks, seeks, or knocks. Somehow the determination to recognize and respond enhances the process of receiving and is called "faith."

The ancient stories demonstrate what practicing therapists have experienced over the years: if a client is not involved in his own healing, not much can be done to help that person. Helpfulness that sparks responsibility empowers growth and healing. Robert Leslie, in his reading of gospel stories through the lens of Viktor Frankl's Logotherapy, envisioned this empowering healing by suggesting that Jesus mobilizes "the defiant power of the human spirit" (Leslie 1965, 24). We will explore empowering healing further below, but first let us observe helping that does not empower.

C. S. Lewis has immortalized the disempowering helper in his character of Mrs. Fidget, "who died a few months ago. It is really astonishing how her family have brightened up."

Mrs. Fidget very often said that she lived for her family. And it was not untrue. Everyone in the neighbourhood knew it . . . "What a wife and mother!" She did all the washing; true, she did it badly, and they could have afforded to send it out to a laundry, and they frequently begged her not to do it. But she did. There was always a hot lunch for anyone who was at home and always a hot meal at night (even in midsummer). They implored her not to provide this. They protested almost with tears in their eyes (and with truth) that they liked cold meals. It made no difference. She was living for her family. She always sat up to "welcome" you home if you were out late at night; two or three in the morning, it made no odds; you would always find the frail, pale, weary face awaiting you, like a silent accusation (1960, 73–75).

Following his brilliant description, Lewis summarizes his point, "This, as we saw, is a Gift-love, but one that needs to give; therefore needs to be needed" (ibid., 76). Lewis has aptly described what has more recently been called by popular psychology the "co-dependent." The co-dependent is a helper who is as dependent upon being needed by someone as the alcoholic is dependent upon alcohol.

Indeed in recent years, popular writers from the various Twelve Step programs have issued stern warnings about the dangers of being too helpful, of doing too much to assist a loved one and thereby inhibiting suffering persons from coming to terms with their suffering, from reaching a point of determination from which they can become responsible for their own lives. Certain kinds of helpfulness prevent assumption of responsibility and further disable the sufferer. That is, being too helpful can inhibit another's ability to respond to a difficult situation. Alcoholics Anonymous, which proved itself early as an effective means for reaching problem drinkers, has stressed this wisdom from its inception. Many years back A.A. developed Al-Anon, a program designed to counsel overly helpful spouses and family members and teach them to "detach," to give up behavior that essentially demeans the alcoholic while assisting him or her to continue drinking.

The following life story illustrates the dangers associated with being too helpful when dealing with a person who needs to take responsibility for his own actions. Daniel Smith, a problem drinker, promised to take his wife, Debbie, to dinner for her birthday. On his way home from work he stopped in at his favorite bar for a drink and completely forgot his promise. When he returned home at eleven o'clock, he found his wife waiting up for him—she was hurt and angry. She scolded him and a fight ensued, during which he vomited all over the bathroom floor and passed out. She cleaned up the mess and got him to bed. She had trouble sleeping and in the morning again broached the problem, but with the help of the alcohol he did not remember the incident at all. His parting shot on leaving for work was, "With such a bitch for a wife, no wonder I drink!" Another day his drinking binge was particularly extreme and his wife was especially helpful, he was too hung over in the morning to go to work, so she called in to say that he had the "flu." Later in the day he complained that she "treats him as a child." Absolutely no amount of talking, reasoning, or scolding on her part made any impression.

This is not an unusual story for those who have lived or worked with addiction, but the wife's brand of helping is a very different model from the one Jesus teaches in the New Testament stories we just explored. The alcoholic is correct: his wife does treat him as a child. And her care-taking prevents him from coming to terms with his problem. Daniel is protected from needing to "ask, seek, knock." So what does Al-Anon suggest? First, that Debbie not plan around Daniel's reliability, that she either plan something else for her birthday or when he fails to appear, that she call a friend and celebrate in another way. Second, it suggests that should she remain at home until he returns, she might go to bed or otherwise find ways to entertain herself. Then when Daniel vomits all over the bathroom and passes out, she should leave him right where he is. When he wakes up, he will be a step closer to Bartimaeus by being able to recognize he has a problem for which he must seek help. Al-Anon's "tough love" advice to this wife is "detach." Let Daniel come to his own conclusion. Nagging is a form of helplessness that stems from an addictive need to be helpful. Obsession with straightening out another person is never helpful and often underscores problems in one's own life. There is not really much love in addictive over-helpfulness, rather there is a desire for control based on deep-seated fear and inadequacy.

Mrs. Fidget and Debbie Smith may appear to be extreme examples, and the solution from Al-Anon may seem shockingly cold. But these people's experiences are probably closer to ours than they may initially appear. In experiments with young children, researchers have noted that infants and children are extremely sensitive to distress in other people, particularly their parents. In fact, small children are often troubled by suffering in another person. Some of us have been in a church nursery when one child begins to cry; the other children become distressed and may also begin to cry. Observation of this fact has led a number of research psychologists to question the egoism in Freud's theory and in the suggestion of social Darwinism that only the fit survive. Martin L. Hoffman, having executed a series of studies, proposes instead that altruism is not just a socially learned response, but a biological component of human nature observable in infants as young as one day old (Hoffman 1982, 282–83). In fact, this biological altruism has a great deal to do with the flexibility and cooperation that is necessary for our species to survive (Hoffman 1981).

As we saw in chapter 2, children have been known to misbehave in order to attract attention to themselves and distract their parents from having a quarrel (Griffin 1982, 121–23). Psychiatrist Joseph Weiss[3] elaborates this demonstration of empathy, "A child may come to condemn himself for what is generally thought of as a normal, acceptable wish or developmental goal if he infers, whether or not correctly, that by attempting to satisfy this wish or reach this goal he may threaten his all-important ties with his parents" (1986, 49). Two other clinicians observe that a child may completely distort his personality in an effort to comfort and nurture a severely troubled parent (Feiner and Levenson 1968). This acute sensitivity to distress in others, "biological altruism," theorists suggest, is an inherent part of human survival.

I propose that not only do children and infants experience a biological empathic concern for another's distress, but that adults also experience it. Biological empathy or altruism is indeed a fact of human nature. We are all distressed by the suffering of other human beings, and probably that of animals and the ecosystem as well. In order to survive amid the sad-

ness of the world, we may employ denial, blot out our awareness. On an individual level, we have a deeply inherent longing to comfort and support. This impulse has both potential
for building community as well as danger for desiring control.
For example, a culturally recognizable method of offering
comfort to a crying child is to hold her, pat her, and say,
"There, there, don't cry." Indeed, this response to our inherent
empathy essentially strives to create a safe environment for
ourselves. We comfort so we can feel more comfortable. We
might assume that we must have the answer to the other person's problem, and set out to fix or control that person, sometimes with urgency, again so that we can calm down. When
this human impulse is combined with Christian vocation,
helping can become grossly disempowering.

Christians who have understood helpfulness, sometimes
against all odds, as an inherent part of God's call, have struggled to discern genuine God-inspired, hope-filled helping
from dependent over-helpfulness. Sacrificial giving has long
been understood to be part of Christian maturity. Have
churches, then, in the very act of encouraging service as part
of religious development and spiritual formation actually encouraged needy giving, giving based more on unreflective biological empathy than on genuine helpfulness?

At this point, it is important to understand the word *responsibility* as I have been using it. Responsibility is an ability to
respond. In popular conversation *responsibility* implies duty,
law, virtue, or goodness. It is a term associated with chosen
ethical behavior. If indeed *responsibility* refers to duty, C. S.
Lewis's Mrs. Fidget would feel right at home. Duty to family,
after all, was her life. And if *responsibility* involves virtue and
goodness, Debbie, the wife of an alcoholic, virtuously cleaned
up the mess when he vomited and, out of the goodness of
her heart, called his work to say he had the flu. But the responsibility I am considering is not our responsibility as
Christians to be helpful, which will be discussed fully in chapter 7. It is not our obedience to law or custom. It is not our
unconscious response to biological empathy. The question
here is whether or not our helping enhances responsibility in
the one who receives our service. In other words, we must
determine what kind of helping is really helpful.

H. Richard Niebuhr in his book on Christian ethics, *The Responsible Self,* considers responsibility as conscientious adherence to law, but also notes that laws are sometimes unjust, citing the Civil Rights movement in the United States. African-American citizens broke unjust laws in our southern states, thereby setting the stage for revision of these laws. "Rules," writes Niebuhr, "are utilitarian in character; they are means to ends" (1962, 55). Citizens working for a common good may also devise a standard for responsibility. But Niebuhr suggests an alternative theory of responsibility as "*response* to interpreted action upon us." Niebuhr says, "Responsibility lies in the agent who stays with his action, who accepts the consequences in the form of reactions and looks forward in a present deed to the continued interaction" (ibid., 61, 64). In the light of this definition, we recognize clear responsibility in the actions of the Civil Rights workers, who protested, demonstrated, and went to jail. In like manner, we recognize irresponsibility in the actions of the alcoholic who drank and did not accept consequences for his actions. For the Civil Rights workers, their faith, risk-taking seeking, asking, and knocking made them well and brought them closer to enjoying the just society for which they longed. In this sense, they wisely employed biological empathy. Conversely, the alcoholic sought only to avoid all suffering. Ironically, he fled into a psychological isolation where he punished himself cruelly.

But Niebuhr takes his theory of responsibility as ability to respond a step further, tying it to the nature of God whom we know in Jesus:

> The God to whom Jesus points is not the commander who gives laws but the doer of small and mighty deeds, the creator of sparrows and clother of lilies, the ultimate giver of blindness and of sight, the ruler whose rule is hidden in the manifold activities of plural agencies but is yet in a way visible to those who know how to interpret the signs of the times (ibid., 67).

Unless there is faith, there is no healing. Unless we are willing to risk everything, buck the crowd as Bartimaeus did, and break the law as the hemorrhaging woman and the Civil

Rights workers did, we will not improve. Unless the pain of our longing drives us to ask, seek, and knock, there will be no real healing. Likewise, if we reach out to help others in our Christian vocation of caring only to assuage their pain, we rob them of the agony that becomes the faith responsible for genuine healing. We are only helpful if we spark in another the ability to respond. Otherwise we yield to the temptation to be God, as the alcoholic's wife did, controlling our loved ones' lives in hopes that they experience no pain. That is, we misuse our biological empathy and comfort others to reduce our own anxiety. Ironically, as we rob them of their action, we rob them of the image of God within them.

When we examined Jesus' helpfulness in the Marcan stories, we observed his pattern of encouraging adult-to-adult dialogue while respecting the petitioners' request for help. In John, we find a story with a different pattern: the healing of an invalid at the Pool of Bethzatha in John 5:2–18. At the Sheep Gate by the pool, Jesus comes upon a man who has been ill for thirty-eight years. Characteristically, he respects the invalid's choices. "Do you want to be made well?" Jesus asks (Jn 5:6b). But the man knows the rules for healing and knows the situation is hopeless. It is useless to respond: "Sir, I have no one to put me into the pool when the water is stirred up; and while I am making my way, someone else steps down ahead of me" (Jn 5:7). Uncharacteristically, Jesus heals the man, ordering him to get up, take up his mat, and walk. Indeed, the man responds and finds himself unbelievably, by the rules of healing that he knows, made well. But responsibility, Niebuhr has cautioned us, that "ability to respond," has consequences, and the responsible agent stands by his action and accepts the consequences. For this Jesus is prepared, but the recently healed man is not.

The story continues: it is the Sabbath, and the man soon finds himself in trouble with the Jewish establishment. Although Jewish law forbids working on the Sabbath, he protests that his healer told him to carry the mat. He refuses to accept responsibility for the consequences of his healing. Finding an illusion of control in his long-established victim role, he reports that Jesus healed him and commanded that he carry his mat. Even when confronted by the authorities, Jesus remains an ethical agent who stays with his action and accepts the consequences: "My Father is still working, and I also am working" (Jn 5:17).

How is it that Christian caring goes awry and becomes an attempt to rescue and control? I propose that an exploration of Christian development toward maturity will assist our inquiry.

The model for development of Christian maturity that I use is one I developed in 1985 with the assistance of seven spiritual directors, four Catholic and three Protestant (Alter 1986).[4] This description of Christian experience was built on a developmental continuum in an effort to capture characteristics of beginning, intermediate, and advanced levels of faith. The religious experience in this study focused on an ongoing relationship with God as person and on ways in which that relationship affected a believer's attitudes and values. It takes into consideration both an inner sense of being drawn to seek relationship with God as well as decisions along the way that enhance the continuing process.

At the beginning level, we found that a lifetime faith journey starts for individuals as they become aware of their family's involvement or lack of involvement with some form of organized religion. In other words, beginning faith is an acceptance of what is.[5] Believers might interpret their early seeking as God's pursuit of them, but since psychologists can only describe what we see happening externally, we would say that individuals move from acceptance of what is into a more active mode; they begin to show an interest or vague curiosity in more explicit personal faith, or perhaps they demonstrate a real seeking. Sometimes the seeking becomes extreme: an existential discomfort or internal and external stress. There comes a point of decision: conversion for the evangelical followed by the glow of first love and vigorous enthusiasm. For Catholics, there is a call to commit to discipline, a decision to frame one's entire life with faith. A period of vigorous enthusiasm ensues. Individuals are caught up in excitement, swept by feelings that there is so much to learn and so little time. It is a period marked by impatience and distinct lack of compassion. Individuals at this point have difficulty separating personal projects from genuine concern for others and authentic self-giving.[6]

Four of the seven spiritual directors involved in developing this theory marked as a point of extreme difficulty the transition from beginning to intermediate stages of Christian maturity. The four suggested that in order for one to progress into mature Christian faith, one needs to establish one's ego and a strong sense of self (see chart 1—charts appear at the end of this chapter).

At the beginning of the intermediate stage (see chart 2) another spiritual director joined the first four in emphasizing one's need for a strong sense of self, which is followed quickly by the second step in which the "pain begins." I suspect that steps one and two in the intermediate stage of Christian development are really closer together than our language implies. But let me first explain my use of the word *self*. Taken from Arthur Reber's *The Dictionary of Psychology*, in which he includes six definitions of *self*, I have chosen definitions 1 and 4. Definition 1 views self "as inner agent or force with controlling and directing functions over motives, fears, needs, etc." Definition 4 treats self "as synthesis, as an organized personalized whole" (1985, 676).[7] This self recognizes itself as separate from others and able to reflect on its own behavior and feelings. Self, therefore, is separate, and has both history and responsibility. This is the self which Niebuhr says is able to respond, ask, seek, and knock. It is the self of Bartimaeus, who bucks the crowd; the hemorrhaging woman, who dares to touch a rabbi. Self as agent can both achieve and fail, exist alone and participate in community. This description of self relates to our understanding of Mahler's theory of psychological birth. A child begins to recognize that it is separate from the mother, but does not yet grasp the individuated ability to be both separate and also participate in community. From this we can recognize that the empathic infant's distress comes from global discomfort in another's pain. The infant cannot yet achieve separateness and would comfort another in order to be comfortable.

A believer's first real grasp of God's love, "conversion," as it is sometimes called, yields ecstasy, union with God, and a sense of wonder. We are swept up, drunk with God. Much like the experience of the practicing toddler, we are not only wonderful and know God to be wonderful, but we know the truth. We have a full handle on knowledge of good and evil, and we are ready to "help" everyone with our knowledge. And if the human potential movement idealizes the narcissistic toddler, many churches idealize the new convert. We have already observed the popular assumption that understands the joy and confidence of the narcissistic infant as "normal" for human life. In like manner, many churches assume that Christian life retains the ecstatic joy and confidence of recent conversion. Unfortunately some church members are made so uncomfortable with the intermediate stage of soul searching that they have labeled it "backsliding" or the "cooling of our first love." As maturity begins to develop, frightened believers may grasp at legalism with lots of right answers and truncate the painful journey into deeper trust and greater vision. Becoming an "adult" is no easy matter. The process is remarkably like rapprochement: we must experience our separateness, our vulnerability, our finitude, our fears, and our doubts. It is not a matter of developing confidence and pride as our culture suggests, but rather evolving humility and trust (Kramer-Rolls forthcoming). Real helpfulness only begins after a more painful and profound knowledge of self.

Enthusiastic new believers gradually recognize that conversion has not solved all their problems as they imagined it would, and pain begins. The pain—shame, abandonment, and humiliation—flood in like a baptism. We are immersed, baptized into experiential knowledge of our finitude. From there we are led into the wilderness, and as spiritual directors explain, "imperfections are noticed." A developing Christian begins to have a greater realism about self, begins to notice that healing and learning to love take time. There is a "real awakening to the illusions of life," a period of "dying" or "letting go." How like rapprochement: the practicing toddler gradually becomes aware that he is not almighty. Two spiritual directors observe that a period of dryness ensues: a "dark night."

Flora Wuellner remarks that although the quietness of God is very uncomfortable to the believer, the time is not barren. "It is like hibernation; the cubs are born then, you know." She explains that people need particular guidance through this time so they do not worry that they have lost their faith.[8] This period in growth of faith also passes, and individual believers find themselves more grounded in and more accepting of their finitude: they "accept limitations," now having a "critical self-awareness." They are more willing to "accept light and dark" in themselves. They no longer cling to a need to deny their imperfections. They begin to integrate parts of their lives as well as beginning to appreciate values from their families of origin. It is in this way they begin to achieve a self.

The spiritual directors wisely observed that this time of painful soul searching does not happen only once, but many times. Self continues to strengthen throughout our lives only through painful surrender of narcissistic illusions of power, perfection, privilege, and control. Only these surrenders, which usually feel like a death, make room available for God.

It is now with a more fully finite sense of self that individuals are ready to surrender to God. Far from a convert's early demands for perfect union and solace, for rescue from pain, intermediate believers understand God as working in the midst of struggle, and far from the desperate efforts to earn value by perfectionism of some sort, they have deepened their ability to accept themselves as valuable, achieving an identity as sinners accepted by God. At this point, God begins to direct, and as Christians become increasingly identified with Christ, more authentic concern for others ensues. Hence, if the beginning stage of Christian development ends with a tyranny of enthusiasm that lacks compassion, the intermediate stage ends with a humility and self-understanding that embodies compassion.[9]

What, then, is helpful, and how do we proceed toward empowering help? The wise therapist knows that most of us, even those seeking help, do not really want to change. Most of us probably would prefer that the world change to make our lives more comfortable. Or perhaps we hope the therapist will perform some magic to make us happier. The human spirit often longs to be taken care of, longs for the rosy fantasy of perfect happiness in union with someone where we are recognized as wonderful and rescued from pain. Unfortunately there is also a tendency within us to misuse biological altruism, which makes us uncomfortable when other people are suffering. We can be easily drawn into protecting, rescuing, or controlling another so we can feel better. We can easily be tempted into a form of helping that does not empower.

The following story helps explain how easily biological empathy can draw us into unhelpful helping. Martin, a professional word processor at the University of California, had just broken up with his girlfriend. A bit paunchy for his thirty-six years, he sat miserably on my couch barely lifting his eyes. He explained sadly that "this always happened with women." He did not know what was wrong. He had even been engaged once, and his fiancée left him, too. In fact, he was not happy with much of his life. His immediate boss was unfair to him, expecting too much and paying too little. His roommates did not understand that he needed more quiet from ten o'clock on so he could sleep. Even people in his church did not really understand him. He had thought that this girl . . . he trailed off.

As I sat listening, I felt wafts of helplessness drift by. Although I experienced them as my helplessness to assist him, I knew I was probably picking up his own feeling about life. Although his friends experienced him as demanding and childish, he saw himself as life's victim. He was not his own agent. He had come to see me in some faint hope that I could do something to make him happier. Truly there was much within me, my biological empathy, that wanted to comfort and reassure him, but I knew that comfort would demean him. It would only be a futile effort to comfort myself. As much as he sought solace, it would not bring out his ability to respond. It would not enhance the Bartimaeus within, the responsible self. I knew that I would struggle to help him enter maturity. I would accompany him, kicking and screaming, through rapprochement with all its attendant fears and rages. And in the end, I would know with Jesus that his faith had made him well.

Nina's was another story. At a communication skills workshop I conducted for a nursery school her daughter attended, Nina asked several pointed questions. Toward the end of the session, she mentioned quietly that she often felt sorry for herself. When I followed up her remark with a phone call, she explained that four years before she had been diagnosed with cancer, lymphoma. She had been pregnant at the time, but had had to sacrifice that baby for chemotherapy so she might live for her then one-year-old daughter. She desperately wanted to live until her daughter, Erika, graduated from high school.

Nina joined a women's growth group, and in addition to providing warmth and support for other participants, she shared with us the intricacies of living with cancer. She astonished us with her observations, "Isn't the world beautiful? Have you noticed the crab apple trees are blooming?" At one point a depressed friend came to visit. Heading off on some errands, Nina had a sudden premonition and returned to the house in a rage. "You were going to kill yourself, weren't you," she demanded. He concurred. "How dare you?" she raged. "How dare you even think of it when I'm dying!"

On another occasion she explained to her growth group, "Erika brings me back to reality. I got word from my doctor that the cancer had moved out of remission. I was so upset that I left the front door open when I went for the full report. When I came home, Erika confronted me, 'Mom, what were you thinking about? You left the door wide open!' It was a relief to return to the ordinary."

Before long it became apparent that Nina didn't need the group; she really had nothing to work on. The "self-pity" was reality-based, genuine grieving for the life she was losing. She left the group, but I maintained contact as she lived her dying. She spent her eight years of limitation and illness making a scrapbook of cards for her daughter, honoring the occasions she would not live to experience. When at last melanoma was added to the lymphoma and Nina lost her hair to chemo treatments, she wore a knit brown angora hat. One month before she died, having always loved a bargain, she went in a wheelchair to a department store sale for "one last fix." In her final month, she wrote a letter to her daughter, then nine, rejoicing in their good times together and bidding her good-bye.

In the end, Nina died easily and quickly, deeply trusting her relationship with God. We learned a great deal from her about integrity and responsibility. Nina was a responsible self. She lived with vigor and joy, responding to her circumstances. For those of us who knew her, we can only attest that her life was abundant.

It is common for us as human beings to feel like victims in some area of our lives, to feel helpless and to complain as if we have no choice. To the extent that we embrace this role and try to avoid or deny the pain in our lives and our ability to respond to it, we set up patterns that make everything worse. Jesus, demonstrating God's priorities, heals by calling us out of a victim role, by appealing to a responsibility inherent in us. Jesus calls us to name our suffering, to decide what we want, and to seek healing. With this accomplished, he marvels and says, "Your faith has made you well."

As Christians, empowered by God, we have no choice but to be concerned with human suffering. Our very existence becomes a vocation of concern. Learning to be a healing friend through Jesus' example enables us to empower rather than rescue. This saying taken from a poster posits the essence of Christian helping:

> *A Friend is someone*
> *Who by what he/she*
> *Thinks of you*
> *Obliges you to be*
> *Fully what you are.*

Christian Development in Three Stages

Chart 1

Beginning Stage

   I. Acceptance of what is, religion as given by family of
       origin. (Hall)
     Interest, vague curiosity, real seeking. (Hazzard)
     Existential discomfort, internal and external stress. (Hiles)
  II. Decision:
     Conversion, enthusiasm. (Wuellner)
     Commitment to discipline. (O'Toole)

 III. Enthusiasm, excitement, impatience, not much
       compassion. (Wuellner)
     Difficulty separating personal projects from genuine
       concern for others and authentic self-giving. (O'Toole)
     Needs to establish ego, strong sense of self. (Hiles,
       Hazzard, Houdek, O'Toole)

Chart 2

Intermediate Stage

I. Strong sense of self. (Houdek)
  Strong self-image, more independent in a good sense.
    (Hazzard)
  Beginning to know self in a significant way. (O'Toole)
  Beginning to identify own values from those of family.
    (Hiles)

II. Pain begins; notices imperfections; greater realism about
    self.
  Finds healing, learning to love takes time. (Wuellner)
  Real awakening to illusions of life; very uncomfortable; a
    "dying" or "letting go." (Hiles)
  Period of dryness, "dark night," hibernation, quietness of
    God. (Wuellner, Hazzard)

III. Accepts limitations: critical self-awareness, accepts light
    and dark about self, does not need to deny them.
    (Houdek, Hazzard)
  Integration of parts of life. (Hazzard)
  Appreciation of values from family of origin. (Hall)

IV. Surrender to God. (Hazzard, Houdek)
  God seen as working in midst of struggle. (Hazzard)
  Learns to see self as valuable then as a sinner accepted
    by God. (J. Chinnici)
 V. God begins to direct. (Hazzard)
  Increased identification with Christ. (Houdek, J. Chinnici)
  Actions in line with Christian values and Scripture.
    (O'Toole)
  Greater certainty about will of God and more authentic
    concern for others. (O'Toole)
  Ability to transcend difficulties and live meaningfully.
    (Hall)

6

The Danger of Certainty

We have observed Jesus' practical psychology emerging from a very different culture and yet still appearing remarkably at home in contemporary times. We have noted Jesus' compassion for the human dilemma in his enthusiastic offers of forgiveness and his efforts to return the law to its original intent. We have traced the human longing for control, for right answers, for safety by our own hands, for being as God in knowing good and evil. We have noted that the holiness for which we strive, God in all graciousness has already granted. This holiness in which we stand contains a vocation of caring, but it is a caring that empowers, but does not rescue. We now pause at this point to note Jesus' treatment of certainty. In some ways what follows is a summary—a chance to examine the style of Jesus' psychology inherent in our previous discussion rather than continuing with its content. The quality of paradox that we observe here will inform our future exploration.

In his ministry, as we have observed, Jesus retains a quality of unexpectedness that disrupts anxiety-generating systems of right and wrong. Marcus Borg portrays the system of Jesus' day as one of "rewards and punishments, righteous and unrighteous, deserving and undeserving." Recognizing people caught in blind systems of certainty, "anxious to receive what they believed they deserved, anxious about holding on to what they had, anxious about social approval" (Borg 1987,

102, 107), Jesus confronts, jolts, and subverts those systems. Jesus' unexpectedness is so consistent as to suggest that certainty based on human systems of merit is not only a blindness but also a danger. Jesus' approach to healthy personality contains this disruption of systems, and I have struggled to convey this in teaching.

In an adult church school class, I tried to replicate something of the unexpectedness of Jesus' teaching with an exercise. On the board I listed a few of Ben Franklin's familiar maxims but left out their endings: "A stitch in time . . ." "Early to bed, early to rise . . ." "Waste not . . ." "A bird in the hand . . ."

Then I invited the class to add endings, and they droned in unison the familiar words: "A stitch in time saves nine." "Early to bed, early to rise makes a man healthy, wealthy, and wise." "Waste not, want not." "A bird in the hand is worth two in the bush." Next, I erased the endings once again and asked them to make up new ones. After a few moments of silence, they began inventing: "A stitch in time saves embarrassment." "Waste not, recycle." A college student ventured, "Early to bed, early to rise makes a man's woman go out with other guys." Members of the class began to giggle. "A bird in the hand would probably like to get away." They picked up "Once upon a time" and remembered other endings: *Once Upon a Mattress,* a play; "Once upon a midnight dreary," from a poem by Edgar Allan Poe; *Once Upon an Apple Tree,* a children's book by Maurice Sendak. Interrupting the hilarity, I asked them if they had noticed a change in atmosphere as they added the different endings. They reflected that the familiar was boring. It was also tediously moralistic. "It's like being nagged by your mother to clean your room," someone suggested. The new endings, they decided, allowed them to hear the sayings for the first time in years. Adding them was fun, energizing, playful. Then one brave individual ventured, "It also feels a little dangerous. Like we are doing something wrong when we change the endings." At that point we had a chance to examine the unexpectedness of Jesus' teachings and its impact long ago and today.

As with Franklin's maxims above, familiarity with gospel sayings and stories can rob us of the frequent element of surprise. Many of us have known the stories since childhood, hearing sayings preached as proverbs and parables taught as allegories, each with its own easily summarized moral lesson. That they were astonishing to first-century audiences and that they continue to encourage revolutionary protest in the name of justice and human dignity throughout the world today is almost unseemly. The sayings of Jesus can become dangerously familiar, barely heard by sleepy worshipers at Sunday morning services. Indeed, some of us needed seminary New Testament classes to exhume the sayings and stories and return them to their original jarring unexpectedness.

Occasionally, the fresh eyes of an unchurched person, or of a youngster from a church that uses the Bible sparingly, upon encountering the stories for the first time bring to awareness the hyperbolic quality of Jesus' teachings. One nine-year-old in a fourth-grade church school class stumbled upon Matthew 7:3–4. "'Why do you see the speck that is in your brother's eye, but do not notice the log that is in your own eye?'" she read aloud. "Huh? What's this?" "Or how can you say to your brother, 'Let me take the speck out of your eye,' when there is a log in your own eye?" "Oh! I get it!" she announced triumphantly to the class. "Don't be so busy telling someone else what's wrong with them that you miss what's wrong with you! Hey! That's good! Let's see what else is here."

After even a superficial reading of the Gospels, a few sayings catch us very much as they did that nine-year-old: "For those who want to save their life will lose it, and those who lose their life for my sake, and for the sake of the gospel, will save it" (Mk 8:35); "But many who are first will be last, and the last will be first" (Mt 19:30); "Whoever wishes to be great among you must be your servant, and whoever wishes to be first among you must be your slave" (Mt 20:26–27); "Love your enemies and pray for those who persecute you" (Mt 5:44); "Blessed are the meek for they shall inherit the earth" (Mt 5:5).

Each saying has an unexpected turn. Whereas the sayings of Ben Franklin carry a pithy moral from conventional wisdom, something to live by, Jesus' sayings leave us startled, puzzled. Like the class's rewritten proverbs, Jesus' sayings catch us off guard, force us to hear them. They move directly against natural tendencies toward self-preservation and certainty, against that which makes good sense. What does it mean to save one's life by losing it? To save one's life, one needs safety, nourishment, nurture, success. It is Abraham Maslow with his "hierarchy of needs,"[1] not Jesus of Nazareth, who makes sense. What does it mean to seek greatness by becoming a slave? If nothing else, this is a strike against equal rights for those who have "slaved" while others have become rich on their labor. If one chooses to be great, one should accumulate money and power, prestige and position, television acclaim. Stock market kings and television stars make sense, not Jesus.

Jesus' other sayings are just as challenging to conventional wisdom. Jesus not only disrupts its humanly self-righteous certainty, he attacks it. Systems of certainty based upon human achievement or human status are not only questionable, they are dangerous. Jesus' arsenal of attacks on these systems is easily demonstrated. Speaking to an audience who equates God's rule with military might, Jesus announces the kingdom not as "a [walled] city set on a hill," therefore invulnerable and protected, or "the cedars of Lebanon," symbols of sturdy endurance, but in these ways: "The kingdom of heaven is like yeast that a woman took and mixed with three measures of flour, until all of it was leavened" (Mt 13:33); "What is the kingdom of God like? . . . It is like a mustard seed that someone took and sowed in the garden; and it grew and became a tree, and the birds of the air made nests in its branches" (Lk 13:18–19).

There is no question that Jesus is talking about power. Who can stop the action of yeast or the mystery of seeds sown in the ground? But for those expecting military might, a show of sovereign power, ultimate protection, liberation, and return to Israel of her national identity, Jesus' words must have been astonishing and disheartening. If we see ourselves as oppressed victims, as people in first-century Israel had good cause to do, and expect rescue by conventional means of power and might, we are likely to be startled by Jesus' insistence that God's power is already constantly present. Once we realize the nature of God's power, we are stripped of our righteous assumption that we would and indeed should be rescued. Essentially we must relinquish our hope of receiving special favor through our own merit and let go of the idea that all "those other people" will get what they deserve. Jesus

teaches us about God's power, but it is a power that subverts
expectation for special treatment. Jesus' parables subvert our
expectations.

Biblical scholars tell us that Jesus' use of the parable is the
ultimate example of the way he surprises his listeners because
his parables subvert and reverse the hearer's chosen world
view.[2] A parable ordinarily is a teaching tool that explains the
unknown in terms of the known. "The kingdom of God,"
therefore, which is unknown, is typically explained in terms
of the known. Most of his audience would equate the kingdom of God with military power. The kingdom of God is as
invulnerable as a walled city built on a hill or as mighty as an
army with many banners. The comparisons Jesus chooses,
however, are unconventional—leaven, a mustard plant, a
woman searching for a coin or a man for a sheep—and they
shatter the expected image of power and majesty.

Jesus not only taught with parabolic sayings and stories, his
life too contained a similar parabolic unexpectedness. He
lived in a manner that astonished and disturbed, that sub-
verted the established sense of honor and dishonor, of purity
and impurity. Jesus ate with the wrong people in a culture
that viewed table fellowship as a symbol of deep intimacy. He
invited himself to dinner with Zacchaeus, the Roman tax collector and betrayer of his own people. He accepted the
"wrong people," welcoming a sinful woman from the streets
at Simon the Pharisee's home. He praised a centurion, an offi-
cer of the occupying army, for his faith, and when he selected
a model of kindness he chose a Samaritan, a member of a
hated, heretical people. The terrible and awe-inspiring
Yahweh, whose name the Hebrews did not dare pronounce,
Jesus addressed as "Abba," an endearing term. Basically, Jesus
was the wrong kind of messiah. Burdened by Roman occupation and beleaguering fears of abandonment by God, Israel
yearned for a messiah, an earthly king with military might.
One can therefore imagine how the people responded to this
Jesus, "a man of sorrows and acquainted with grief," the "suffering servant" of Isaiah, who achieved victory through death
on the cross.

At the same time that Jesus dismantled existing status and
honor systems through his welcoming of the "wrong people,"

his treatment of the "right people"—that is, the scribes and Pharisees, priests and Levites, honorable and religious, those of good family—presents another surprise. We have already noted that Jesus accepts a woman from the streets while dining with Simon the Pharisee, but he also confronts Simon for the intentional snub in attempting to shame Jesus through inhospitality. In Jesus' parable of The Good Samaritan, society's presumed good people act badly, and the presumed bad people act virtuously. On other occasions, Jesus simply calls good people "white-washed tombs." He says to his disciples that unless their righteousness exceeds that of the scribes and Pharisees they will never enter the kingdom of heaven. Observing the continuously unexpected turns in Jesus' life and teachings, one can see how family therapist Jay Haley might interpret them as power tactics in his essay, "The Power Tactics of Jesus" from his book by the same title. But were these surprises indeed power tactics? Was Jesus scoring personal or political points in an intellectual or even therapeutic contest?

Bruce Malina's description of the first century's cultural understanding of honor and dishonor can help us as it has in chapters 1 and 2. As we noted there, this peasant society understands honor to be available in only limited supply, like all goods. Any individual who is not a member of one's extended family is able to take honor away through a series of complex encounters (Malina 1981). Something as innocuous by our standards as receiving a gift can diminish one's own honor and that of one's family. Some of Jesus' verbal sparring with Pharisees is his method of managing the honor challenges. But there remains a deeper question: do Jesus' paradoxical subversions have any purpose beyond cultural maneuvering? Marcus Borg suggests they do, and that by these actions Jesus radically disrupts an anxiety-ridden conventional wisdom of rewards and punishments. If we begin with Borg's understanding of Jesus' message—God is essentially compassionate, "nourishing, life-giving, 'wombish'"—then the parabolic quality of both his teachings and his life begins to make practical sense. From this perspective we can again explore the sayings we listed above.

In the Gospel according to Mark, Jesus says, "For those who want to save their life will lose it, and those who lose their life for my sake, and for the sake of the gospel, will save it" (Mk 8:35). In the first-century Mediterranean world, however, saving one's life would surely involve preserving one's honor, and thereby one's family's honor and social status. Since honor and influence are understood to be limited, individuals remain anxiously on guard against the possibility of anyone taking away their family honor and prestige (ibid., 90).[3] Preservation of honor demands wariness about actions and challenges that would diminish status in the eyes of the community.

Jesus, going against conventional ideas of honor and status in the community, suggests that the central reality is the ultimate graciousness of a compassionate God, and that those embroiled in conventional concerns of status and honor in order to prove status with God become encumbered with anxiety and hostility. Those who seek control or security through conventional systems of purity and honor are not only personally paralyzed but choreograph their generosity according to the demands of the system. These people eliminate any possibility for trust or cooperation, and certainly are not capable of showing the radical concern for others required by Jesus. Life for people overly concerned with status and honor, therefore, loses openness and compassion in its anxious grasp at certainty and security. As Jesus says, "Those who lose their life for my sake, and for the sake of the gospel, will save it" (Mk 8:35). On the other hand, those who abandon conventional systems of honor and purity to trust the compassion of God open their lives in many astonishing ways. With conventional wisdom thus turned on its head, indeed the first become last and the last first. One who seriously lives out the compassion of God does not worry about status in the conventional sense and therefore may be regarded by those who are concerned about status as despicable and without honor, a slave. Hearers are urged to "love enemies and pray for those who persecute" them. With the central reality of God's love, all are urged to abandon security. It is the meek, not the honorable and the powerful, who will inherit the earth, who will be first in the kingdom.

We, too, embedded in a different culture, have our own "honor" systems, our own methods of determining status and assuming prestige, our own conventional wisdom, our own certainties. Our education or our wealth or our "correct" Christian doctrine set us apart. We are not like those others; we are among the correct. For us as well as those in the first century, Jesus' challenge disrupts: the center of life is God's ultimate graciousness and compassion. It is lavished upon us apart from our deserving. We are invited to abandon our certainties, our security, so that we may inherit abundant life.

The kingdom sayings follow suit. We are no longer observing a kingdom of national dominance and military might; not ultimate protection, but rather an indomitable homey force present and available in daily life, a homey force whose power is something of a mystery and beyond human control:

> The kingdom of heaven is like yeast that a woman took and mixed in three measures of flour, until all of it was leavened (Mt 13:33).

> What is the kingdom of God like? . . . It is like a mustard seed that someone took and sowed in the garden; and it grew and became a tree, and the birds of the air made nests in its branches (Lk 13:18–19).

As the balance between men and women in these images suggests, this kingdom of God is a force that is not built on gender roles and conventions, an observation that offended first-century audiences.

The parable of The Good Samaritan presents an even more powerful attack on human systems of honor and purity (Bailey 1980).[4] Compassion permitted within a system of honor and purity appears heartless, which is one of the key ironies of this story. We are not told the wounded person's ethnic identity, and this, of course, would have provided the impetus for the Priest and the Levite, with attention to purity codes, not to stop. In helping an unconscious person, possibly near death, with neither garment nor accent to identify him, the priest and the Levite would have risked ritual pollution and so refrained.

Jesus' choice of a Samaritan as the good neighbor is also ironic and intensely offensive. Bailey, in an effort to illuminate the hostility Jews felt for Samaritans and particularly the danger the Samaritan faced bringing a wounded Jew to the inn, writes:

> An American cultural equivalent would be a Plains Indian in 1875 walking into Dodge City with a scalped cowboy on his horse, checking into a room over the local saloon, and staying the night to take care of him. Any Indian so brave would be fortunate to get out of the city alive *even* if he had saved the cowboy's life (ibid., 52).

Since Jesus told the story to a lawyer in a Jewish audience, we might presuppose the victim was Jewish. This final parabolic twist suggests that it might be the very person against whom one holds the most intense and "justifiable" prejudice who offers a service most desperately needed. With delicious implied humor, Jesus' story suggests that the certainty to which we cling with whitened knuckles prevents us from receiving intended blessing. The very person from whom we defend ourselves with our systems of certainty is likely to be the person whom we most desperately need. Indeed it is our blind prejudgments that prevent our entering into abundant life.

Hence the unexpectedness of Jesus does indeed have a point and a very explicit one. It is a continual warning about the danger of certainty: a constant disruption of what is presumed deserved, earned, and controlled. It consistently subverts callousness, blindness, and insensitivity. It continually interrupts the anxiety buried in conventional wisdom and offers in its place an assurance of the ever-present graciousness of God. In a word, it is a continuing invitation to live in one's finitude, loved and empowered by God.

What, then, does all this have to say about psychological health and well-being? Although psychologists have not yet arrived at a consistent understanding of mental health, they have identified qualities that attend psychological distress. Sufferers from mental illness, for example, are caught in rigid patterns of control fueled by fear, helplessness, and self-hate. In such distress, we generally find ourselves unable to connect warmly with other human beings and unable to learn from experience. Far from acting fancifully on feelings, at such times we hold our feelings in such tight check that they are beyond our awareness or possible contact. In our heart of hearts many of us believe that feelings will destroy us. At the edge of consciousness we fear an emptiness and rage that threaten our very existence.

Examining the extreme of psychological distress serves a clarifying function here; we recognize a familiar theme: human fear and the longing to be in control, to dominate, to make oneself ultimately safe. Once again we recognize the powerful human longing to be God, our drive to resist finitude. In Jesus' paradoxical treatment of certainty and its self-perpetuating anxiety, he once again invites his followers into the full finitude that he accepted at his baptism and sorted out through his days in the wilderness. He invites them and us into a single certainty, that a compassionate God is the center of reality. If we were to allow Jesus to unseat our security systems, our concrete certainties, in favor of a "Spirit-filled reality," a world in which the final reality is a gracious and compassionate God who alone is in control, would this make a difference? In his jostling disruption of honor-and-dishonor certainty, dramatized in the parable of The Good Samaritan, Jesus poses a significant question: Do our heartfelt righteous certainties and our absolute prejudices wall us off from potential blessing and therefore from knowing the reality of the Spirit-centeredness of our world?

In teaching adult education classes in churches, I have invited participants to imagine themselves as the wounded person in the parable while embracing their community or ethnic identity with all its biases, and to imagine receiving help from someone they would least expect to be helpful. The imaginary stories have been enjoyable, but the ensuing flood of actual parabolic life experiences lent dramatic clarity to Jesus' disruption of status quo as it might appear in contemporary society.[5]

One person told the story of a counselor from a local high school who received word that a riot would break out between rival gangs the following day. With understandable trepidation he and the faculty and staff made preparations to present a calm but firm stand to keep the campus quiet. At 7:30 the next morning as they were taking their stations, a dozen tattooed and leather-jacketed members of the Hell's Angels motorcycle club pulled their motorbikes into the school parking lot. "Oh, no!" The counselor reported feeling, "This is the last thing we need today!" But these citizens, too, had heard the rumor, had recognized the danger, and had come to support the faculty in their effort.

Another person told our group of a young couple from a strong Mennonite congregation in Pennsylvania who had moved to San Francisco following a job. They found a house suitable for themselves and their two children but were not quite able to afford it without renting out a couple of rooms. Through their church they were able to secure two male roomers. One of these young men was delighted, as he told them, to be part of a "real family." He helped with chores, played with the children, participated in family dinners, and was instrumental in creating genuine community. Needless to say, the couple was delighted as well. Only after several weeks did they realize a fact the young man had not attempted to hide: he was homosexual.

Another member of our group talked about a woman with a strong sense of social justice who enacted her concerns in college and graduate school through political action. This woman regularly participated in demonstrations and even attended a sit-in at the president's office. In protest to a racial incident on campus, she changed graduate schools and finished her degree in another state. When a family friend called her some years later, she reported having just become engaged. "How wonderful!" the friend responded. "To whom?" She paused before responding. "Well," she said, "he's a Marine Captain. And more than that, I met him through a dating service." As the friend laughed, the woman paused again before finishing her thought. "God has a good sense of humor."

Human craving for certainty, driven by a partially conscious dread of finitude, is apparently universal. We have seen aspects of it before in our discussion of perfectionism and holiness. We have explored Jesus' insistent disruption of honor and purity systems of his times. We have seen Jesus' abrasive insistence on the God of grace as the center of reality. We have considered examples of contemporary parables in which the disruption of certainty facilitated a particular flow of grace. Yet, we might ask, is certainty dangerous? How might we consider it so?

Human longing and striving for certainty is indeed dangerous. It consistently destroys community, compassion, and
blessing. It can be relied upon to turn good news into bad.
Perhaps this can be most clearly understood through an individual story.

A woman from a warm evangelical congregation sought
counseling because of a crisis in her family. It was very apparent that her relationship with God was central in her life and
that at age fifty, consistent with her lifelong integrity, she
sought my assistance in discovering how she was contributing
to the family troubles and to her own unhappiness.

It became clear that in addition to the warmth of her congregation and the centrality of a personal God in their worship, this church and others to which she had belonged
offered an implied certainty. The idea conveyed was that if
you are a good Christian, if you put God first in your life, if
you have a "quiet time" regularly and read the Scriptures, if
you are involved with church work, if you are submissive to
your husband as a Christian wife, then life will unfold with
unruffled blessing for you and your children. The implied certainty of her church reinforced the implied certainty of her
parental family. As the oldest child she learned to be a very
good girl. If she was a very good girl, did her school work,
was nice to everyone, and did not call undue attention to herself, then everything would go well for her.

Both certainties absolutely forbade that she listen to disruptive feelings. When her husband left for Vietnam, her parents
took him to the airport "so as not to upset" her. She stayed
home and cleaned the bathroom. The pressure was great
enough to prevent her from crying then or grieving later. Having
moved home during his tour of duty, she submitted to family
pressure that inhibited private conversations with him when he
called. When he returned, she endured humiliating failure in
their sexual relationship, his long absences because of work,
and his abrasiveness at her expense in various social situations.

As she raised two girls and one boy, psychology, in a vigorous effort to correct the abuses of organized religion, added
its own certainties. If you are sensitive to your children, if you
use good communication skills, if you do things together as a
family, then your children will blossom into fully functioning,

happy adults. After years of black moodiness that spoiled many family occasions, her husband unilaterally elected to leave and live on his own for a year. She nursed her oldest, then a teenager, through a prolonged illness while also assisting the second child, a boy, with his learning disability. A year after completing college, her oldest daughter confided that her father had sexually molested her as a child. A year later the same daughter confided that she was a lesbian.

Lacking her mother's inhibitions about being noticed, the older daughter spoke freely about being lesbian and, with help from a therapist, confronted her father about his incestuous acts toward her. The father at first admitted a variety of sexual difficulties, then withdrew, filed for divorce, and later remarried. The daughter, who had actively participated in church youth activities and attended a Christian college, experienced withdrawal and rejection from the church. The son, away at college at the time everything exploded, refused to discuss the family situation, elected to remain in his college town for vacations, and left the church. The younger daughter took the father's side. She raged at her sister for alleging that he molested her and at their mother for failing "as a good Christian" to condemn the homosexuality. About this time, popular psychology introduced the mother to the term *codependency* and suggested to her that she was too involved in the lives of her family.

Fortunately for the mother, friends from church with their own intuitive sense of Spirit-filled graciousness rallied to her support, choosing friendship over doctrinal purity. Individuals comforted her at crucial points, providing practical assistance with her move from the family home and a willingness to listen over coffee when the stress was unbearable. Gradually, with much hard work in counseling, the woman became aware of the certainties that had controlled her life. She became distinctly less of a good girl who was nice to everyone. Silenced feelings emerged like Jeremiah loudly proclaiming to Israel that something was badly wrong. She recognized and refused her mother's coercion. She reassessed friendships. She recognized before the divorce proceedings that her husband was not "smarter" as she had always assumed, but that his actions were mean and undermining. Freed from the demand for submission, she became angry, hired a lawyer, and fought for the terms of divorce she needed. Her "prophetic" feelings freed her from psychological certainties. The feelings assisted her dealing with her younger daughter's attacks on her parenting with increasing equanimity and firmness. She refused to be drawn into her son's moody withdrawal from the family. As the certainties dissolved, she gained dignity and quiet command, putting into practice the excellent skills she had developed over many years. Throughout this time God remained central in her life, and the recognition of God's abiding presence in the midst of her suffering increased as the certainties of right theological and psychological doctrine with their guarantees and judgments diminished.

There is no question that certainties are inherently dangerous. Certainty promises what it cannot deliver. Essentially it promises that we can escape from finitude, that we do not have to suffer if only we "do" what a particular doctrine suggests. With false prophets of old, certainties proclaim their message: A person who believes the right thing about God, or has the correct communication skills, does not have problems with his or her family. Those who elect faithfulness to any certainty must always be on guard, ever watchful at church coffee hour for evidences of insufficient or incorrect faith and ever watchful that their performance is flawless. Those who suffer are therefore suspect, and those who do not suffer can never quite relax in a community of love. In fact, suffering folk often find themselves isolated from the "faithful" of any particular theological or psychological system as if they were somehow contagious. No flaw can be admitted in a system of certainty or all of us will confront the terror of our finitude.

God is interested in our ultimate freedom, abundant life imbedded in finitude. The gospel allows us no righteous certainty controlled by our own manipulations. Jesus consistently disrupts certainty with its suspicions and guarantees. He disrupts its self-perpetuating cycle of anxiety and judgment. Instead, he offers an invitation to openness and compassion toward others and blessing for ourselves, an invitation to recognize reality as "ultimately gracious and compassionate" (Borg 1987, 100). He invites us to live by trusting in God and surrendering the illusion of control. His gospel speaks directly to two primary human fears: fear of abandonment and fear of finitude. Wooed by God's longing for relationship with us, we are assured of the presence of the Spirit. Entering into our finitude in all its poverty and suffering, we are invited to see life in light of the resurrection. Our lives and deaths are in God's hands.

A Vocation of Concern

I n the last chapter, we explored Jesus' style of enacting a practical psychology, his continual disruption of human systems of certainty. We also considered the attractiveness of certainty and the accompanying pressure it exerts on human lives. Finally, we suggested that systems of certainty are dangerous. In chapter 5 we considered the caring to which we are called as Christians, and recognized that caring can be a complicated issue. We observed in Jesus a consistent style of caring that empowers rather than rescues. In this chapter we further explore our vocation as a servant community. We address the question, What is our identity of caring that empowers but does not rescue, is wholehearted but not certain?

Concern for others and for the world is a Christian calling. It is vocation and identity. Concern for others, similar to our responding to God's abiding love, is another element of life's meaning. Compassionate concern for others is central to the messages of both the law and the prophets upon which Jesus builds, and the Gospels are full of radical challenges for people to live with active concern.

We have already examined the parable of The Good Samaritan as an example of grace from unexpected places, but—as is more frequently stressed in churches—Jesus ends the parable with a parting challenge: "Jesus said to [the lawyer], 'Go and do likewise'" (Lk 10:37b). We have also seen in Jesus' exposition of the law, the Sermon on the Mount, that he attempts to recapture the fundamental intent of the law as radical graciousness to all human beings, even those with hostile purpose:

> You have heard that it was said, "An eye for an eye and a tooth for a tooth." But I say to you, Do not resist an evildoer. But if anyone strikes you on the right cheek, turn the other also; and if anyone wants to sue you and take your coat, give your cloak as well; and if anyone forces you to go one mile, go also the second mile. Give to everyone who begs from you, and do not refuse anyone who wants to borrow from you.
>
> You have heard that it was said, "You shall love your neighbor and hate your enemy." But I say to you, Love your enemies and pray for those who persecute you, so that you may be children of your Father in heaven; for he makes his sun rise on the evil and on the good, and sends his rain on the righteous and on the unrighteous. For if you love those who love you, what reward do you have? Do not even the tax collectors do the same? And if you greet only your brothers and sisters, what more are you doing than others? Do not even the Gentiles do the same (Mt 5:38–47)?

These radical challenges to live as if the kingdom were already fully present move beyond the conventional wisdom of Jesus' time: beyond exclusive loyalty to family and clan (Malina 1981, 67), beyond concern for purity, honor, and status (Borg 1987, 97–124). In addition, Jesus acts to create family out of radical loyalty to God:

> Then his mother and his brothers came; and standing outside, they sent to him and called him. A crowd was sitting around him; and they said to him, "Your mother and your brothers and sisters are outside, asking for you." And he replied, "Who are my mother and my brothers?" And looking at those who sat around him, he said, "Here are my mother and my brothers! Whoever does the will of God is my brother and sister and mother" (Mk 3:31–35).

Given this understanding of family, Jesus departs from any tradition of limiting concern for others to immediate or extended family. My neighbor is not only the person who lives near, but the person who is in need. My family is not only my blood relatives, but another who loves and obeys God. The world is neighborhood replete with my sisters and brothers, and all children are my children.

Under the mores of "conventional wisdom" one achieves status from giving alms to the poor. But in this vocation of concern, there is no status at all. Charity performed must be done anonymously:

> So whenever you give alms, do not sound a trumpet before you, as the hypocrites do in the synagogues and in the streets, so that they may be praised by others. Truly I tell you, they have received their reward. But when you give alms, do not let your left hand know what your right hand is doing, so that your alms may be done in secret; and your Father who sees in secret will reward you (Mt 6:2–4).

Our vocation of concern is not lost on adult church people to whom I have presented these materials. They understand church as a community that embodies concern for others. It is a forum in which they can discuss altruistic concerns while living in a largely materialistic culture. In essence they recognize their vocation of concern as the fabric of their church membership: concern for those who are part of the church community, for people in need in the local community, and for people in need abroad. When I invited one group to list with me their felt concerns, the list grew rapidly: the homeless, poor children, injustice and war, refugees, schools in the United States, famine abroad, victims of natural disasters. The list was endless. When the flow of suggestions slowed to a trickle, I asked, "Looking at this list, how do you feel?" "Terrible," they told me. "Overwhelmed, burdened, hopeless."

What is it we are seeing here? Did Jesus intend to burden believers with impossible demands, to raise the level of expectations to such heights as to defeat and dishearten his followers centuries later? Is this not the same man who intones:

"Come to me, all you that are weary and are carrying heavy burdens, and I will give you rest" (Mt 11:28)? What can we make of this?

Let us examine some additional incidents from Jesus' life. In the story where he raises Lazarus from the dead, Jesus is fore-warned by Mary and Martha that his friend their brother is very ill. "Accordingly, though Jesus loved Martha and her sister and Lazarus, after having heard that Lazarus was ill, he stayed two days longer in the place where he was" (Jn 11:5–6).

Jesus' negligence is not missed by the sisters, each of whom upbraids him for his slowness in coming: "Lord, if you had been here, my brother would not have died." We are told, "When Jesus saw her weeping, and the Jews who came with her also weeping, he was greatly disturbed in spirit and deeply moved . . . Jesus began to weep" (Jn 11:33, 35). As ever, Jesus is enigmatic. If he is confident in his ability to raise Lazarus, why does he weep? If he loves these people so much, why does he wait so long to come?

Again Jesus baffles us in the temptation story. "He fasted forty days and forty nights, and afterwards he was famished" (Mt 4:2), we are told, and then he is approached by the tempter, who offers him an opportunity that most of us, com-piling our chalkboard list of concerns for others and the world, would have been sorely tempted to accept: "If you are the Son of God, command these stones to become loaves of bread" (Mt. 4:3). The use of the plural is significant here. Loaves are not only for appeasing Jesus' hunger, but to feed the hungry. Ordinarily the idea of being able to saunter out to a public park in some urban center and announce to the homeless, "Come and eat. These stones have become bread" or to do the same for refugees huddled in camps in a foreign land would readily tempt our good intentions. But Jesus has another agenda: "It is written, 'One does not live by bread alone, but by every word that comes from the mouth of God'" (Mt 4:4). Jesus, as we have noted before, refuses to be tempted to be-come more than finite. His finitude, like ours, is empowered by God. Though alleviation of hunger and poverty are con-cerns, they are not ultimate concerns. He does not allow the Accuser to demand that he become more than human.

I think of the faces of well-fed but worried and burdened participants in adult church school classes, the seminarians, the graduate students I have taught. Together and in isolation from one another, we have heard the demand of the Accuser, "If you are really a Christian, why have you not done more? Why are there still hungry in the world? Why have you not alleviated injustice?" We are called to a vocation of concern, but only within the confines of finitude. We are called as well into our powerlessness: powerless against the death of our beloved friend Lazarus and the grief of his family and friends, powerless against our many inabilities to meet the needs of the world as we observe them. When we hear from God, "Whom shall I send?" we may with trembling respond, "Here am I. Send me." We may indeed put our shoulders to the tasks, to our jobs, to our lives, trusting that powerless as we feel, we are indeed empowered by the God who loves us and calls us to serve. That somehow what we are called to do in this vocation of concern will bring blessing through our own limited power in harmony with a power beyond our own for those we serve. Somehow we are involved in bringing about the realm of God that is yet to come.

But there is a cost, a messiness, about our vocation of concern. We will not only experience our own powerlessness and the consequent pain, but we will be touched by misery. As Jesus mourned for Lazarus, we will mourn; we will feel to the depths of our finite beings pain of concern for the suffering world. This we cannot escape. Indeed we must not escape. In the midst of these feelings, strident voices within us will proclaim that all we are doing is not enough, it is fruitless, being finite is not sufficient. We feel compelled to somehow find a way of becoming God in order to fix the world. The strident voices will demand that we either fix the problem or abandon our concern entirely. Forget it. Let someone else handle it. This hurts too much.

We come, then, to another collection of puzzling sayings: the Beatitudes, particularly those that directly address the vocation of concern with its cost in human pain: Matthew 5:4, 6, 7, 9, and 10. "Blessed are those who mourn, for they will be comforted." Happy are we who mourn? What an outrageous thought! But our mourning like Jesus' mourning is an appropriate and necessary response to suffering. Concern of necessity draws us into contact with anguish in the world, and in our finiteness we too will experience human grief. We too will

grieve for the cities of the world as Jesus grieved for Jerusalem (Mt 23:37; Lk 13:34). If we are aware of it, we may recognize that we grieve as well for the world that might be if
justice were established, or we grieve for the imagined safe
world of childhood that we have "lost."

Psychology has long told us that it is only those who grieve
the deaths and losses in their lives who will find comfort.
Sufferers who cannot grieve or who are so afraid of becoming
overwhelmed by their grief that they refuse to grieve are
haunted and controlled the rest of their lives by their unre-
solved losses. Some become ill from ignored and festering
grief. But we are called not only to mourn our losses, but with
Jesus to mourn the anguish of the world. And we shall be
comforted. How? we want to ask. "That doesn't make sense."

People commonly assume they cannot bear to mourn the
suffering of the world: "I don't want to hear it." "I hate to
have all that sad business dumped upon me." Or, "I don't
want to see a play with a sad ending; I prefer happy things."
Or the reverse: "I don't want to burden my friends with my
troubles." It is easy to imagine here Ernest Becker's assertion
that as a species and as a culture we put maximum effort into
denial of death, denial of suffering, denial of powerlessness
(1973, 1–8). And indeed we expend energy in denial of our
finitude. Jesus sees it differently. We are not only called to
mourn, we are invited to recognize that the blessing is in the
grieving, blessing is in the finitude. As we grieve, we will find
ourselves comforted by God in the community of those who
also have the courage to accept Jesus' challenge.

In the Beatitudes we are not only invited to mourn for the
suffering of the world, fully embracing our sense of finite
powerlessness, but we are challenged to ponder the meaning
of yet another paradox: "Blessed are those who hunger and
thirst for righteousness, for they will be filled" (Mt 5:6).
Blessing lies directly within our willingness to own a passionate desire for justice and mercy in a world of violence,
hunger, and deprivation. We know in our hearts, of course,
that this hunger and thirst for righteousness is foolishness.
Nevertheless, if we are called to mourn with all our hearts, we
are also called to hunger and thirst. A just world becomes
nourishment, food, and drink. When we are not afraid to rec-

ognize in ourselves this hunger and thirst in a suffering and unjust world and have the courage to live in the powerlessness of our finitude, we will find that we have surrendered our petulant demand for perfect safety. At this point, pockets of God's righteousness can appear to us. Having surrendered our longing for personal heaven with ourselves in control, we are freer to recognize the Spirit working beyond our wisdom in the world around us. We experience having eyes to see the realm of God now present.

In a world that is often cruel and warmongering, we are called to identify happiness with mercy and peacemaking. "Blessed are the merciful, for they will receive mercy . . . Blessed are the peacemakers, for they will be called children of God" (Mt 5:7, 9). We certainly recognize the peacemakers and the merciful among us, with a silent prayer of gratitude. The insistent courage of people like Mahatma Gandhi, Mother Theresa, Martin Luther King, Jr., and Desmond Tutu provide for us longed-for examples of God's mercy and call us into mercy and peacemaking of our own in whatever capacity is available to us. The merciful and the peacemakers carry a naive confidence that the gospel challenge to concern for others may be taken seriously, and in solidarity with their courage, we continue in our own efforts. That we might receive mercy or be called children of God remains part of the mystery of our Spirit-filled call.

The conventional wisdom of our culture has implied that good intentions and righteous actions are rewarded with honor and status. Our folk tales are full of valiant heroes honored in the cause of good. Comic pages, television stories, and movies remind us of the daring deeds of heroes like Robinhood and Superman, eventually honored or even routinely counted on by ordinary citizens. Contemporary writers provide many more, sometimes misunderstood or mistakenly charged, but in the end properly recognized and honored. If we have not learned from the suffering and deaths of our prophets and our peacemakers, Jesus in another beatitude sets the record straight: "Blessed are those who are persecuted for righteousness' sake, for theirs is the kingdom of heaven" (Mt 5:10). We are called to concern in the midst of our powerlessness, and the result may well be persecution.

Even persecution cannot deter the peace and joy inherent in the integrity of pursuing justice for all.

We will feel our concern in the powerlessness of our finitude. We will continue to be called to mourn, to hunger for righteousness, to be merciful, to be peacemakers, to persevere even in the face of persecution. We will participate in all this in the midst of finitude, clearly unable to fix all for which we feel grave concern, and precisely in the midst of this ambiguity, will we find and receive blessing: peace that passes understanding.

Jesus' practical psychology has something to offer to our understanding of health and well-being. Does a vocation of concern set in the powerlessness of our finitude enhance our lived perception of abundant life and mental health? Yes, without question. It has been observed that abusive treatment of others destroys the abuser as well as the abused. In the same way I suggest that concern for others is inherently healthy, a blessing. This claim can be statistically supported.

In a 1985 study with a sample of 125 randomly selected participants from two Presbyterian churches, I demonstrated a positive correlation between faith as experienced through concern for others and mental health. The Christian Experience Inventory (CEI), a measure of Christian experience and maturity based on five faith scales, and the Brief Symptom Inventory (BSI), a measure of mental illness symptoms, were correlated. The scale that most consistently and strongly correlated with low scores on appearance of mental illness symptoms was Experience of Faith through Concern for Others (Alter 1989). In other words, those participants who had a strong experience of faith through concern for others generally showed better mental health, sometimes statistically significantly better, than those who had weaker scores on that scale, who did not experience their faith through concern for others.

We have recognized in chapter 5 that helping others can be complicated. In some instances helping can be a dependency of its own, an "addiction." That is, we can become so intent on helping others that we may use our concern to hide from our own finitude, and thereby avoid our own need to grow and change. We have seen that when we use helping to deny our finitude, we rescue and therefore demean those we had originally intended to empower. In this way we rob them of their dignity by failing to expect them to respond to their situation on their own, the responsibility or "faith" Jesus affirmed in those whom he healed. How then can concern for others be good for us?

Vocation of concern, as we saw in our consideration of the Beatitudes, is a transformation of attitude: If we are to respond to Jesus' call to concern for others and for the world, as we have said, we will experience solidarity and therefore we will simply feel more pain, mourning over human suffering as well as hungering and thirsting for righteousness. These experiences are the natural result of approaching finitude in human beings. The tragedies of the world, the misery of other people, will touch our hearts. The willful evil of persons in power will evoke in us the grieving we witnessed in Jesus' grieving over Jerusalem. There will also be times when mercy and peacemaking are clearly dangerous. We may well be willfully misjudged and "persecuted for [our] righteousness" (Mt 5:10).

It is enormously tempting to barricade ourselves against stories of suffering and pain in others. There can be an illusion that misfortune is somehow catching or that we must have a solution to an individual's situation. If we cannot become as God and fix the problem, we might be inclined not to want to hear about it. From this place it is easy to see those who suffer as pathetic and helpless, and this understanding of them in itself overwhelms and frightens us. The very status of privilege makes us into perpetual victims who require others to treat us as fragile.

Anna Ornstein, a major contributor to the school of self-psychology, challenges the fragility of the privileged among psychotherapists. She alleges that therapists have proposed the so-called "Holocaust survivor syndrome"[1] because they are unable to endure hearing the Holocaust stories. "The profile of the survivor has been sketched as that of a man or woman whose psychological wounds had never healed" (1985, 99). These wounds were assumed to have been passed on to succeeding generations. However, studies done in 1981 and 1983 "could not find significant differences in psychopathology between the children of survivors and their control group" (ibid., 103). Ornstein feels that "the understanding of the mode of adaption to the conditions as they existed during the years of persecution and victimization constitutes 'the missing link' that could meaningfully connect the survivors' pre-Holocaust past with their recovery and adaption to a new life" (ibid., 107). She suggests that small social groups that formed spontaneously had a great deal to do with successful survival. "These groups provided the setting in which everyday human affects, hostilities, jealousies, loyalties, love, and caring could be experienced and expressed. There were honest fights, disagreements, and reconciliations within these groups, and there was fierce commitment and much sacrifice, similar in intensity to those experienced in family life" (ibid., 107, 109–10). Ornstein also suggests that the horrors of the camp become distorted without reference to the context of the camp. For example, being tattooed, a horror to the outside world, within the camp context meant that one would be allowed to live and was a cause for rejoicing. Even the newcomer's task of cleaning the latrines had its privileges:

> It was essential to conquer one's disgust at the smell emitted by the load. The discovery that performing this job gave one the privilege of physical inviolability was cause for rejoicing. Such was the stench of the crews working in the sewers removing sewage that SS officials, instead of reacting "normally," ran off holding their noses. The conclusion to be drawn was clear: the Scheisskommando . . . was relatively seldom exposed to beatings and searches, and this created further practical opportunities for adapting to the camp (ibid., 112).

Ornstein suggests that the problem is sometimes not with the patient so much as it is with the therapist: "What is crucial in Danieli's report is that these reactions by therapists and researchers were not created by their patient's transferences, these were not true countertransferences. Rather, these were reactions to the events of the Holocaust themselves. . . . On the whole, survivor-therapists, and their children as therapists, appeared to handle their affects somewhat better than did nonsurvivors" (ibid., 124–25).

Ornstein's excellent article has a significant point for us. When we wish to draw away from human suffering, we are likely to set up a self-protective system that makes us psychologically ill. Whereas when we accept Jesus' challenge to a vocation of concern in the midst of our finitude, we make a choice for greater experience of empathic suffering, but also richer health and deeper joy.

Indeed, as we are willing to participate in the suffering of others, we will begin to witness a power and a courage in context that was previously invisible to us. This is remarkably easy to demonstrate. One woman in an adult church school class began work helping disabled people with recreation activities. She found the attitudes of determination in these people, nearly all of whom were confined to wheelchairs, so rewarding that she felt she was receiving more than she was giving. Another person from this same class trained for a hospice program for the dying, saying all the time that she was not sure she would actually do it. When she did at last take a case, she found the experience of caring for a man through his dying was profound and moving.

Even under the worst of circumstances, enacted service to others can bring unexpected blessing and possible life change. In one example, a woman who accidentally hit and killed a man with her car at a moment when she was blinded by the sun was sentenced to fifteen hundred hours of public service at a community health clinic where doctors and nurses volunteer time and anyone is welcome to receive health care. She was independently well-off and had not done much volunteer work in her life. The spirit of the volunteers and the care that was offered amazed her. Her required service commitment broke open her life to the possibility of genuine wholehearted giving.

In another case, a young man at a local community college responded to a call for volunteer tutors willing to teach learning disabled students. He had been feeling depressed and thought that working with someone worse off than he was would make him feel better about himself. He was astonished to find the learning-disabled man with whom he worked was full of joy and eagerness for learning even though he was not able to do well in school. The disabled man offered his tutor renewed hope for his own life. Even such reluctant giving can bring unexpected blessing and potential change. What might happen if we deliberately step beyond our comfort level in concern for others?

Willingness to leave the small area in which we may feel safe and enter into solidarity with suffering changes us. It draws us away from the human tendency of fearful denial of that which we cannot fix. We must face and participate in caring for an imperfect and suffering world. These experiences change our understanding, deepen our compassion, and make of us world citizens.

In some cases the results of embodying concern for others with all its attendant pain are remarkable. One devout Sufi traveling on a bus in the 1970s with her husband and other members of their commune drove through Afghanistan and India. As she encountered villagers and city dwellers along the way immersed in poverty, she felt the pain of her own helplessness and inwardly made a vow, "I promise that I will not forget you. I promise that meeting you will sometime make a difference." Some years later after the commune had settled in California, she flew down to Mexico on vacation. As she was leaving the plane, she felt God ask her to find out about the area's Guatemalan refugees. At their guest house, she asked the hostess. "Oh, yes," the woman replied, "there are two settlements of refugees here and I know the woman who works with them." That began indigenous work not only with refugees in that area but eventually with widows in the homeland itself. "If I can do something like that," she said to me, "truly anyone can." Perhaps the only people who can begin such work are those willing to endure the pain such a call from God entails. At this writing, this woman is president of an international service organization.

Participation in the world of the powerless has a possibility of transforming our understanding of graciousness: the graciousness of the poor and powerless, such graciousness as that on which the Old Testament law was founded, for it was founded on the experience of a people who had once been enslaved. An English teacher in an adult high school, white and a product of general privilege with a college education, was committed to teaching the relatively poor in a city setting as a result of her sense of Christian vocation. Over ten years she found herself touched in surprising ways. At one point a student told her that he had jury duty and would miss the rest of the week. He was a quiet, unremarkable student with unremarkable grades and an unremarkable contribution to class discussion. When he returned two days later, she was surprised. "Hi, Mr. Jones," she greeted him. "What happened to jury duty?" An understated black man slightly older than herself, he replied quietly, "I was seated on a jury for a robbery. I told them I couldn't do it. I knew someone had to, but I just couldn't. There were too many times as a kid when I might have done the same thing." The young teacher was profoundly touched. It was as though she had met the toll collector of Jesus' example, who prayed in the temple but felt himself unworthy to lift his eyes to God (Lk 18:9–14).

An American who had achieved a college education by personal struggle and the G.I. bill served for four years in India as a Presbyterian mission worker, as the business manager for a boarding school. Twenty years later when he returned to the school, he was not on the campus half an hour before the Indian staff began to recognize him. "Sir," one man said, "remember, you hired me!" Another reminded him that he had helped them establish a credit union. A third reminded him that he had raised their salaries. Never mind that that had been twenty-three years earlier. Out of the complaining affluence of the United States, the enthusiastic appreciation of long-past favors deeply touched him. Before he and his wife left, the staff who had known him held a dinner in his honor.

Recognizing our lives as a vocation of concern has the possibility of transforming us. When we leave a designated area of relative safety to face without denial issues of suffering, poverty, and death, we open ourselves to appalling pain and unimaginable blessing. But I think there is a second way in which living a vocation of concern transforms us: in this time of rampant careerism when individuals nervously refuse to commit to one career for fear of cutting off the possibility of deeper satisfaction from another (Bellah et al. 1985, 119–20), calling to a vocation of concern is a call to the integral significance of all life. Since every life is called to a vocation of concern, all living has significance. Robert Fulghum demonstrates this possibility in his description of a driver's education instructor:

In most American high schools there is someone who teaches driver training. The top sergeant of automotive boot camp. Thankless task, a low-status job, about in the same league with the typing teacher as far as the faculty pecking order is concerned. The driver trainer is something of a non-person (1988, 69).

Fulghum, however, discovers that the driver training instructor at the local high school is a much-loved and widely respected person. The kids call him Obi Wan Kenobi, the wise one from *Star Wars*. On investigation, Fulghum discovers Jack Perry: "You wouldn't notice him on the street or pick him out of a police lineup for ever doing anything remarkable." Perry's distinction was apparently the way he understood his contribution:

"—Guess this sounds presumptuous, but I think of myself as a shaman—I help young men and women move through a rite of passage—and my job is getting them to think about this time in their lives" (ibid., 70, 71).

His unselfconscious concern for kids and community transforms a low-status job into a vocation.

Langston Hughes, in his superb story "Thank You, M'am," addresses the vocation of concern. The story opens with an attempted mugging, eleven o'clock at night on a city street. A fifteen-year-old boy attempts to snatch a purse from a large middle-aged woman on her way home from work as a hairdresser in a downtown hotel. The purse strap breaks and the boy loses his balance and falls on his back. "The large woman simply turned around and kicked him right square in his blue-jeaned sitter. Then she reached down, picked the boy up by his shirt front, and shook him until his teeth rattled. As she had him pick up her purse, she said, 'Now ain't you ashamed of yourself?'"

The woman neither screams nor calls the police. Rather she puts a half-nelson around the boy's neck and drags him down the street as she continues on her way home. "You ought to be my son, I would teach you right for wrong," she tells him. "Least I can do right now is to wash your face. Are you hungry?

"No'm," said the being-dragged boy. "I just want you to turn me loose."

"Was I bothering you when I turned that corner?" asked the woman.

"No'm."

"But you put yourself in contact with me," said the woman. "If you think that that contact is not going to last awhile, you got another thought coming. When I get through with you, sir, you are going to remember Mrs. Lucella Bates Washington Jones.'"

The woman takes the frightened boy home to her modest rooming house, turns him loose, and orders him to go to the sink and wash his face. Her toughness combines with a human concern: "'Let the water run until it gets warm,' she says. 'Here's a clean towel.'" She asks the boy his name and shares her supper with him. Clearly not one to indulge in denial, she asks him why he tried to snatch her purse. When he tells her he wanted a pair of blue suede shoes, she reflects, "'I were young once and I wanted things I could not get.' There was another long pause. The boy's mouth opened. Then he frowned, not knowing he frowned."

The woman said, "Um-huh! You thought I was going to say but, didn't you? You thought I was going to say, but I didn't snatch people's pocketbooks. Well, I wasn't going to say that." Pause. "I have done things, too, which I would not tell you, son—neither tell God, if He didn't already know. Everybody's got something in common" (Hughes 1971, 25–29).

In a very true sense the meal of lima beans and ham and cocoa was communion for these two strangers. In the end the woman gives the boy ten dollars for his blue suede shoes, leads him to the front door, and bids him good night while saying, "Behave yourself, boy!" Too shy even to say thank you, the boy continues to look up at the woman on the stoop as she shuts the door. I see this as a Zacchaeus story: the apparently unworthy has been returned and welcomed through table fellowship into human community. Mrs. Lucella Bates Washington Jones's unselfconscious human concern opens the door of healing and new possibility to a potential mugger.

We are called by Jesus into a concern for others, a call that represents our identity and vocation. Our life meaning is to respond to God's love and to carry that love, centered in our finitude, to others in the world. This vocation of concern transforms our lives: it draws us out of fragile privilege into a solidarity of grieving for the suffering of the world and hungering for its correction. This solidarity brings us into contact with those in need and our understanding of their context transforms pity into empathy. Our service to others becomes a blessing to ourselves. Secondly, since vocation of concern is a central tenet, it transforms our lives in yet another way. Instead of searching for a vocation that might offer meaning, we carry with us Jesus' calling to a vocation of caring and concern in all aspects of our lives. The very way we envision our lives, then, has inherent meaning.

A Place for the Prophetic

W e have noted the tenderness of Christianity in our consideration of forgiveness, received holiness, and concern for others. We have also observed toughness through law, responsibility, and Jesus' insistence that we human beings surrender our demand for ultimate control and safety. We have marked Jesus' parabolic teachings and lifestyle that consistently disrupt our expectations. At this point I want to address a most difficult part of practical human psychology: our ability to welcome our God-given prophetic voice.

Prophets have always been a problem for the communities in which they live, and prophets in a psychological sense are no less troubling. Biblical prophets, we understand, deliver a message of criticism and hope in an atmosphere of numbness and death (Brueggemann 1978). They proclaim a God of freedom committed to truth, compassion, and justice against a culture that has defined God as servant to the status quo. The prophetic message addresses a deadened present with implications for an energized community in the future. The oppressed receive their message with amazement; the privileged with resistance. Jesus, in full prophetic tradition, upbraided the use of law for status and privilege over against the original meaning of law: living God's inbreaking compassion and forgiveness "as if" the kingdom were fully present. Sinners received him with joy as he invited them into the kingdom of God's love; the privileged arranged his execution.

Such a prophetic voice resides within each human psyche, a voice both critical and energizing. The God of freedom committed to truth, compassion, and justice proclaims criticism and hope against our deadened cultural or personal status quo. These pronouncements terrify us and threaten us with ensuing vitality. Like biblical prophets, they are called into action against our will to pronounce judgment and proclaim hope. Walter Brueggemann, who defines the task of prophetic ministry as holding "together criticism and energizing," observes, "We know, of course, that none of us relishes criticism, but we may also recognize that none of us much relishes energizing either, for that would demand something of us" (ibid., 14). Like messages from the prophets and from Jesus, these voices disrupt a wearied deadness of usual living within us and suggest possibilities for new and vigorous life. But we may well be unnerved by their urgency.

The psychotherapeutic community has long concerned itself with human resistances to the power of this energizing, invasive force. Without our theological context, psychotherapists identify this force with emotion or feeling. They describe such consequences of stifling it as psychological numbing, repressed memory, passivity, helplessness, and depression. In this chapter we explore the action of this enlivening function, its definition and history in psychology, and our understanding of its action as we recognize it in Jesus' life and teachings. In addition, we explore in our own lives a place for the prophetic.

One way to begin our discussion is to observe the struggle in an individual life. Patty spent our first three sessions enthusiastically extolling the Christian life and explaining to me how important it was to her to be seeing a "Christian counselor." A nineteen-year-old sophomore at the University of California at Berkeley, she had had a conversion experience at a youth camp when she was sixteen. Her sister Mary, four years older, had been heavily involved with a Christian college group, and was now married and living in the area. Apart from the two sisters, no one in the family was particularly interested in Christianity and the others, parents and a younger brother and sister, were even a little embarrassed that the oldest two had "gotten religion." I continued to raise questions

and push a little bit to interrupt Patty's enthusiastic mono-
logue. There was something that troubled me about it. As I
listened, I had an inexplicable sensation of sadness.

Session four began abruptly. Patty sat in pained silence for
a few moments before blurting out, "I got a problem." I sat
with her in the pause. She pursed her lips and perhaps her
entire face in her struggle to find a way to phrase her
thoughts. "I think I'm a terrible Christian," she said, her face
anxious. I sat with her again in the pause waiting for her to
sort out her reflection. Suddenly she burst into tears, "I can't
love my sister. She says that charity begins at home and that I
am hateful. She says that I may think I'm a good Christian just
because I go to church and to Bible study and to prayer meet-
ings, but that I'm really horrible, condemned by the Bible because I don't listen to her." Patty broke into terrible sobs, and
sobbed for several minutes with her head in her hands. When
she looked up again, face streaked with tears, her face re-
sumed its tense, anxious look. "What can I do?" she asked
with a depth of sincerity.

"Could you help me clarify a couple of things, Patty?" I
asked.

She nodded, watching me, large-eyed, with a respectful
desperation.

"You're having trouble loving your sister and you feel that
is condemned by the Bible?"

She nodded.

"Can you tell me, when you listen deep down inside to
your feelings, what do they say about your last encounter
with your sister?"

"Actually, I was supposed to go home—you see, my family
lives in Oakland—Sunday for dinner, but Mary was going to
be there with her husband. I just couldn't bear the thought of
seeing her, so I called my mom and told her we had an emergency meeting in our living group—I live in a Christian community—and I couldn't come." She burst into sudden tears
again, and buried her face in her hands. Without lifting her
head she asked with clear agony in her voice, "What can I do?
What can I do? I just couldn't bear to see her and I lied." Her
crying became a wail, helpless and miserable.

As she became quiet, I said, "Patty, that resisting feeling has a very important message for you, a message you can't make be quiet. It is just that insistent."

She looked up at me again, puzzled and silent.

"Can you tell me what these feelings were saying to you that made you call your mom? They gave you some urgent message. Could you be very respectful of them and listen to what it was?"

"But they were terrible feelings. I lied because of them."

"I know, and the fact that you lied scares you a lot. I can see that. But the feelings themselves were trying to give you an urgent message. Could you listen to them with genuine respect, even if they scare you, and tell me what it is you hear?"

"I can't love my sister the way I'm supposed to," Patty looked at me with desolation.

"Help me understand what that means to you. What is it that you are seeing?"

Patty began to cry again with deep pain. "I can't love her. I can't love her. I just can't love her!"

"Is that what you're hearing from those feeling? Feelings like these are like Jeremiah the prophet. They insist on saying something we don't want to hear. Sometimes we feel they are wrong. Can you tell me what those intense insistent feelings are saying about your sister?"

"She says she's only trying to help me, that she tells me the truth in love like a Christian sister."

"It sounds as though she criticizes you a lot, and justifies it in the name of Christianity. It sounds as though your warning feelings, your internal prophets, are telling you something."

We continued for some time probing the validity of her feelings about her sister. At the end of our session, I suggested that she spend the week listening carefully to what her feelings said about her sister's treatment of her. She was skeptical, but agreed.

The following week, Patty returned with a lot of information. "My sister," she reported with animation, "always has something negative to say about me. Sometimes she criticizes my hair or my dress. Sometimes she asks about my living community and then tells me how we should be different."

"It sounds as though you are your sister's project."

"You know what?" she asked and then continued without waiting for my answer, "she never says anything positive about me or about my friends. Every time I'm around her, I feel a kind of coldness. Actually I can feel a kind of dread."

"I'm beginning to understand why you lied to your mom a few weeks ago."

"Yeah! I just couldn't stand the thought of having Mary pick on me for yet another evening."

"In the name of Christian love?"

"Yeah, isn't that weird? I think she does this criticizing bit with her friends as well."

"Perhaps," I suggested, "your prophetic voices are offering you some very significant information."

Patty, like many people, was unable to receive information from her own feelings, particularly resistant ones. It was spiritually mature, she has understood her church to say, to ignore irritation, anger, or resentment. One must rise above such "negative" feelings. Patty's difficulty, of course, is deeper than her conscious effort to control negative feelings and occurs more broadly than definitions of spiritual maturity in particular churches. Intense emotional reactions of any kind threaten to unsettle our understanding of ourselves and take control of our actions. Mothers caution excited children to "calm down." Like small children on the verge of a tantrum, we may feel that we will disintegrate, that we must protect ourselves at all cost from the power of these emotions. English theologian H. A. Williams captures human anxiousness about intense feeling when he describes joy as "a tricky customer" that can "gate-crash into your life like an overpowering guest who dominates everything and begins to make you feel displaced" (1979, 9). With Patty we might find ourselves, bewildered by an un-planned action, puzzling, "Why would I do such a thing?" It is not surprising that human beings have found feelings a diffi-cult part of finitude and that many cultures dictate control of emotional responses if not outright repression of feelings.

Since its inception with Sigmund Freud, modern psychol-ogy has concerned itself with this phenomenon of tightly con-trolling, indeed blotting out, emotional responses. Initially writing during a period of history that advocated extreme emotional control, Freud addressed a particular result of repressed feeling: loss of memory. Encouraging patients to talk about whatever came to mind, and later employing hypnosis, he hoped to retrieve the repressed traumatic or sexual memory, believing that such retrieval would give patients relief and restore them to health. Indeed, retrieval of memory remains central to contemporary psychotherapeutic work and is, in itself, sometimes healing. But many advances have been made in understanding the function of emotions in personality and the consequences of their repression. A number of theorists have addressed feelings, their importance and their dynamics, and we will examine their descriptions. Some of the theories, embraced enthusiastically, have become popular themes in self-help literature. Some of them have even become trendy. As they have become popularized, the theories tend to promise relief from the anxiety of feelings and imply a promise of ongoing liberation and happiness. The popularized theories become overly optimistic and promise what they are unable to deliver. Ironically, it is precisely against this kind of optimism, false prophecy, that Jeremiah raged: "They have treated the wound of my people carelessly, saying, 'Peace, peace,' when there is no peace" (Jer 8:11). We recognize once again intense human longing for guarantees.

As we address human longing to control feelings and indeed control our universe, we are once again facing a theological concern. In order to receive the information from our feelings, we must also experience our powerlessness against their intensity and with powerlessness comes the threat of disintegration, finitude at its most frightening. Most of us create complex defense systems to shield ourselves from such awareness.

The therapeutic community continues to concern itself with personal feelings, information obtained from them, and the results of repressing them. I will cite a few descriptions from psychological theory that come closest to my understanding of an internal prophetic voice, then I will define the function of a biblical prophet and how that can be seen throughout Jesus' ministry.

Against the disciplined background of the 1940s and 1950s, Frederick Perls introduced Gestalt therapy, a system that understands psychological functioning as a Gestalt, an organized whole. In Gestalt therapy, Perls insisted on integrating all psychological energies, most particularly internal resistances. Observing that human beings became embroiled in internal arguments with themselves, Perls advocated "not resisting the resistances," feeling all feelings, and introduced a form of therapy in which clients acted out their internal dialogues.

Perls's contemporary, Eric Berne, had also observed these internal arguments. Describing personality as being built on three ego states—Parent, Adult, and Child—in his system, Transactional Analysis, Berne suggested that the Parent and Child engage in furious conflicts. During these conflicts, the Parent employs such words as *should, must,* and *ought to,* and the Child, who can also be spontaneous and playful, whines, resists, rebels, and abdicates responsibility. Berne suggested that these conflicts are internalized dramas from childhood and that the Adult ego state needs to mediate between the warring factions. Berne's description of the "Natural Child" who was curious, playful, and spontaneous encouraged awareness of feelings, caught popular imagination, and became romanticized beyond Berne's more complex description of a Child ego state, who also manipulates to gain control.

Carl Rogers represents a third voice encouraging attention to feelings. Through his consistent emphasis on listening intently to other persons, he essentially taught them to listen to their own feelings in a deeper way. Indeed, accurate listening to feelings remains an essential feature of all empathic therapeutic practice.

In the 1960s and 1970s many clinicians used Rogers's empathic listening and combined Perls's Gestalt therapy with Transactional Analysis. These accessible systems became immensely popular not only with therapists but in self-help literature as well. Perls's and Berne's theories joined the human potential movement, where a romanticized search to "free up" the Natural Child, that part of the personality that is playful, curious, and spontaneous, reached epidemic proportions. Listening to feelings became acting on feelings, and "being open." Open expression of feeling became a popular cure for all emotional ills. Feelings themselves became enshrined as ultimate truth tellers in a frantic search for happiness: "If it feels good, do it," proclaimed a poster of that period, portraying a hippopotamus wallowing in a mud hole. Enthusiasts dropped out of jobs, careers, and marriages in search for a popularized promise: lifelong childlike spontaneity. Once the Natural Child was released, the promise ran, we would be confident, happy, spontaneous, productive, and good. Perls's secular "prayer" proclaiming the right to do one's own "thing" without being beholden to anyone gained great popularity (1969, 4).

These approaches, embraced as philosophies of life, gained acceptance as paradigms, but soon proved themselves impossible to sustain. The utopian enterprise collapsed and those who were able returned to former jobs or careers. The character Andre in Wallace Shawn's movie *My Dinner with Andre* brilliantly portrays the apex of these popular approaches: the narcissistic search for self. Independently wealthy, Andre had wandered the world experiencing safe (and expensive) trauma in his pursuit of confidence and spontaneity. He enthusiastically relates experience after experience to his admiring friend, the mundane and materialistic Wally. I include one small segment:

> They had in fact dug six graves, eight feet deep. And then I felt pieces of wood being put on me—I mean, I cannot tell you, Wally, what I was going through—and I was lowered into the grave on a stretcher, and then this wood was put on me, my valuables were put on me, in my hands, and they had stretched a sheet or canvas about this much above my head, and then they shoveled dirt onto the grave so that I really had the feeling of being buried alive. And after being in the grave for about half an hour . . . I was resurrected, lifted out of the grave, blindfold taken off, and run through the fields, and then we came to a great circle of fire with music and hot wine, and we danced till dawn (Shawn and Gregory 1981, 55).

Drowned by the human passion for paradise, the original contributions of Rogers, Perls, and Berne could easily become lost. Essentially, all three men recognized and articulated an important truth: feelings, particularly resistant ones, are a significant aspect of human life that we ignore at great cost.

Emotional truths remain basic elements in the world of clinical psychotherapy. Something as ordinary and as troubling as our emotional reactions to life may fulfill a calling as a prophetic voice. They declare, sometimes obscurely and sometimes clearly but generally with intensity, that something is wrong. They proclaim criticism and hope into a weary personal present.

When I suggested to Patty that she listen to her prophetic voices, my language came close to another system of psychology: a popularized understanding of archetypes in the collective unconscious from the work of Carl Jung. This system was described in chapter 4. As you remember, the collective unconscious ostensibly contains accumulated memories of experiences repeated in human beings over many generations. "Racial memories or representations are not inherited as such; rather we inherit the *possibility* of reviving experiences of past generations. They are predispositions that set us to react to the world in a selective fashion" (Hall and Lindzey 1978, 119). Within the collective unconscious are universal ideas called archetypes, which correspond to human experiences of "mother" or "hero," for example. Jung's theory endeavors to capture the complexity of the human mind and explain cross-cultural human universality. His understanding of the archetypes has caught the imagination of enthusiasts. With an interest in "becoming aware of the archetypes," these individuals are likely to express an interest in dialoging with the "hero," the "shadow," or "the wise old woman." That is, they listen to an internal wisdom that might arise from certain universal human experiences. When encouraging Patty to listen to her "prophetic voices," I was using a metaphorical description of an emotional function but did not intend to identify it with an archetype. In order to clarify my particular understanding of this function, I will rely on expertise from two biblical scholars and one Presbyterian minister.

A popular view that clouds our understanding of biblical prophets and their function claims that a prophet is a seer or fortune-teller. Prophets, some believers assume, predicted disasters and judgments, as well as the coming of Jesus as Christ. Others believe that biblical prophets have described in reliable detail events regarding the Second Coming of Christ and the

end of the world. Writers on the subject of prophecy warn
that this interpretation limits or even trivializes our comprehension of the prophetic. Frederick Buechner, a Presbyterian
minister and writer, with whimsical wisdom corrects this view
in his description of *Prophet:*

> Prophet means *spokesman,* not *fortune-teller.* The one
> whom in their unfathomable audacity the prophets
> claimed to speak for was the Lord and Creator of the
> universe (1973, 73).

That *prophet* does not merely mean *seer* is verified by Joel
Green in his helpful book *How to Read Prophecy.* He clarifies
the nature of the message:

> Often the prophetic message proclaimed a future judg-
> ment or salvation; however, we would be badly mistaken
> if we concluded from this that the prophetic message
> was directed only toward the future. *The cutting edge of
> the prophetic message was the present* (1984, 59).

The message of the prophet is a comment on the present
with repercussions in the future: "In the midst of spiritual de-
terioration and cultural upheaval God raised up spokesmen to
proclaim a needed, fresh, forceful message. This message jux-
taposed warning and encouragement, judgment and hope"
(ibid., 57).

Walter Brueggemann argues that prophecy holds together
criticism and hope in a message of urgency against resistance:

> The real criticism begins in the capacity to grieve be-
> cause that is the most visceral announcement that things
> are not right. Only in the empire are we pressed and
> urged and invited to pretend that things are all right—ei-
> ther in the dean's office or in our marriage or in the hos-
> pital room (1978, 20).

Prophecy speaks out against an accepted reality, a status
quo, a tendency to say that everything is all right when it is
distinctly not all right. We are describing a disruptive voice,

one that speaks a truth urgently in the midst of resistance. The voice is a distinctly uncomfortable one. Buechner reflects this quality: "The prophets were drunk on God, and in the presence of their terrible tipsiness no one was ever comfortable. With a total lack of tact they roared out against phoniness and corruption wherever they found them." He adds with inimitable whimsy, "There is no evidence to suggest that anyone ever asked a prophet home for supper more than once" (1973, 73–75).

If we are to identify the prophetic in our psyches, we must understand that it will present itself as a disruptive element, something in ourselves that we may long to silence or ignore. It will be called into action against our will and will threaten the very integration of our understanding of ourselves and our world. It will roar out against phoniness in our selves and in our community. The prophet in ourselves, like the prophet in the biblical communities and the prophetic voice in Jesus' ministry, is "raised up" to perform this service. In Patty's circumstance, the prophet within roared out against the phoniness of "sisterhood, speaking truth in love" when indeed it was domination and oppression. The warning would not be silenced, commanding her behavior before she had consciously listened. When she honored the message, it called to her attention an abuse that would destroy the relationship if it were not addressed. This was not an insight Patty desired; rather, it presented itself against her will.

Ted's experience had additional elements: economic danger and injustice. At my first meeting with Ted, he was twenty-four and working for a subcontractor handling detail work in a housing project. A cheerful man from an optimistic family, Ted expressed concern over his deepening resentment against his boss. When I asked for additional information, Ted reported a deepening debt as well. Apparently, his boss repeatedly requested that Ted "pick up a few things" for their current job, and then did not get around to reimbursing him. On several occasions the boss asked easy-going Ted to bring money to pay the crew, and again avoided repayment. By the time he raised the issue with me, Ted was ten thousand dollars in debt and smoldering with anger. His optimistic approach to life left him no option to deal with this abuse.

Exploring further, I discovered that Ted was also in a relationship with a woman whom he greatly idealized. She was generally critical of him, consistently finding fault with his lifestyle, manners, and dress. Ted worked very hard at pleasing her, never quite measuring up to her standards.

"What is this like for you?" I asked.

"Terrible," he replied. "I feel angry and depressed all the time. Trapped. That's it. In both situations, I feel trapped. Everything keeps getting worse."

"And you keep on flashing that great smile of yours," I said.

"I know. It's a habit."

"Does Ted get to vote on how things are going in his life? I think he may be disenfranchised."

"No. Everyone else's opinion seems more important. A lot of times I don't think I know what my opinion is."

"And so your girl beats on you and your boss rips you off. That must feel terrible."

"Terrible," he repeated pensively.

"Your internal prophetic voices aren't getting your attention. And as a result, you are in grave danger. I wonder what would happen if you truly heard them out?"

"I feel angry," Ted said thoughtfully.

"And what is that about?"

"I've got to stop this from happening to me."

"That sounds wonderful, Ted. My guess is that you also know what steps you need to take to stop it from happening. Let's see if we can discern those steps."

And Ted indeed did know. We began to design a plan for him to follow, listening together to his own prophetic voices.

Joel Green writes, "What we find, then, is that persons become prophets through God's initiative. God chooses whomever he will, calling those who are ill-prepared and unworthy (sinners, that is), and by an act of grace appoints them as bearers of his word" (1984, 52). Buechner echoes this understanding in his definition:

No prophet is on record as having asked for the job. When God put the finger on Isaiah, Isaiah said, "How long, O Lord?" (Isaiah 6:11) and couldn't have been exactly reassured by the answer he was given. Jeremiah

pled that he was much too young for that type of work
(Jeremiah 1:6) . . . Like Abraham Lincoln's story about
the man being ridden out of town on a rail, if it wasn't
for the honor of the thing the prophets would all have
rather walked (1973, 75).

Something within ourselves is called into action no matter
how ill prepared we feel we are, and no matter how unworthy or suspect that portion of our personality stands in our
opinion. The warning is God-given and is likely to roar out
against our will in some form of resistance: anxiety, resentment, irritation, or anger. Most likely we will muster our best
forces in the name of "healthy psychology" or "mature spirituality" into silencing them.

The status quo within our very bones is a status quo of ultimate control. Brueggemann identifies this:

> The deadliness among us is not the death of a long life
> well lived but the death introduced in that royal garden
> of Genesis 2–3, which is surely a Solomonic story about
> wanting all knowledge and life delivered to our royal
> management. That death is manifested in alienation, loss
> of patrimony, and questing for new satiations that can
> never satisfy, and we are driven to the ultimate con-
> sumerism of consuming each other (1978, 50).

The prophetic voice within us is called to cry out against
the demand for "royal [and unjust] management," that demand
for perfect control that ultimately enhances inner emptiness.
In the following case, the justice required involved ethical
treatment of a subordinate.

Julie, pressed by a new superior to promote an individual
with less experience and seniority over another whom she felt
better deserved the promotion, found herself anxious and unable to sleep. Following the wisdom of popular psychology,
she accused herself of being "too compulsive" to leave work
at work. Her worried husband offered mini-lectures on turning off the internal television, but nothing worked.
Psychology offered only an individualistic framework; Julie
resonated with concern for her work community. There was

no way to persuade herself that the administrative action expected of her was all right. The issue was much deeper than compulsive attention to work or popular psychology's methods of leaving work at work. A truth within her was roaring out against pressure to minimize her integrity. She was caught between her political position with a new, unsympathetic supervisor who frankly attempted to coerce her agreement and to compromise her sense of justice to those she supervised. The prophetic voice within loudly resisted. It communicated by embodied visceral distress.

Julie described to me her "compulsive" work-related insomnia, but upon hearing the story, I confirmed that she was trapped. That the issue was not compulsive inability to relax, but violation of her basic integrity, her fairness and loyalty to her staff as a supervisor. Julie essentially hungered and thirsted for righteousness. We discussed it for some time and clarified the issue. On returning to work, Julie told her supervisor that she personally recommended the more senior person, but acknowledged that the decision was the supervisor's and not hers to make.

There are, of course, those who have heard and responded to their prophets' cries for righteousness, fully understanding the biblical intent. Some of these have attained international recognition for positions they have taken against injustice, and their obedience to God's call changes the world. One of these, Martin Luther King, Jr., using biblical imagery with clear comprehension, cried out for justice against the status quo of racial violence and discrimination in the United States. Among the protesting crowd were his fellow clergy. In his letter to them from the Birmingham jail, he addresses their criticisms:

> I am in Birmingham because injustice is here. Just as the prophets of the eighth century B.C. left their villages and carried their "thus saith the Lord" far beyond the boundaries of their home towns, and just as the Apostle Paul left his village of Tarsus and carried the gospel of Jesus Christ to the far corners of the Greco-Roman world, so am I compelled to carry the gospel of freedom beyond my own home town. Like Paul, I must constantly respond to the Macedonian call for aid.

Moreover, I am cognizant of the interrelatedness of all communities and states. I cannot sit idly by in Atlanta and not be concerned about what happens in Birmingham. Injustice anywhere is a threat to justice everywhere. We are caught in an inescapable net of mutuality, tied in a single garment of destiny. Whatever affects one directly affects all indirectly. Never again can we afford to live with the narrow, provincial "outside agitator" idea. Anyone who lives inside the United States can never be considered an outsider anywhere within its bounds (1964, 77).

Our prophets cry out and frighten us. They do not ask our permission, and they will not be silenced. Like Jeremiah, they cry out against false comfort, "They have treated the wound of my people carelessly, saying, 'Peace, peace,' when there is no peace" (Jer 8:11). The internal voices interfere with our peace of mind, our sleep, our ability to relax after work. They refuse to affirm that all is well when all is not well. They have a quarrel with the world. Buechner reminds us that "deep down it is a lover's quarrel. If they didn't love the world, they probably wouldn't bother to tell it that it's going to Hell. They'd just let it go. Their quarrel is God's quarrel" (1973, 75). We ignore them at great cost.

So the prophet within us is called into action in spite of ourselves. It introduces truth that has to do with justice, a hard truth that brings a quarrel with life's status quo, perhaps our personal status quo. To speak from the prophetic impulse is to bring about a quarrel, but it is a lover's quarrel. It aims to bring about healing.

In Patty's experience she felt internal resistance to her sister's "truth in love" criticisms. As long as the behavior continued, Patty found herself increasingly falling into patterns of avoidance. She had a quarrel with her sister's right to be an authority on her life, and the relationship would be increasingly broken until expressing this hard truth interrupted the status quo. In Ted's experience, the resisting feelings warned him of emotional and financial oppression, and in Julie's they communicated patent injustice with which she was expected to corroborate. Initially, we do not want this voice that begins an urgent quarrel out of love. From our perspective it does not feel loving but we ignore it at great peril. Walter Brueg-gemann defines the prophetic vocation clearly:

> The task of prophetic ministry is to nurture, nourish, and evoke a consciousness and perception alternative to the consciousness and perception of the dominant culture around us.
>
> I suggest that the dominant culture, now and in every time, is grossly uncritical, cannot tolerate serious and fundamental criticism, and will go to great lengths to stop it. Conversely, the dominant culture is a wearied culture, nearly unable to be seriously energized to new promises from God (1978, 13, 14).

9

An Approach to Evil

W e have noted that our psyches are equipped with an early warning system, a prophetic voice that alerts us to potential danger for ourselves and for others. This prophetic voice is called into action often against our wills and can easily frighten us into denying or suppressing it. Sometimes, in the name of Christian maturity, churches encourage members to ignore these voices that often present themselves as anger, resentment, or irritation. When we ignore or suppress our prophets, we are in grave danger. We impair our ability to discern threats to our own well-being as well as injustices to others. In refusing the wisdom of our prophets, we may be tempted to deny evil entirely. Indeed denial of evil is endemic in United States culture today.

Psychology, ironically, has had little to say about evil in human personality. In fact, it has said less and less about evil over the course of its hundred-year history. This has been particularly true in the United States since the 1950s, when theorists and practitioners began to take issue with Freud's pessimistic view of human nature. Since that time scholars have postulated a series of strongly positive understandings of human nature, assuming that in a normal state the human psyche and the human body should be free of pain. Popular culture consequently began idealizing children, and therefore ourselves, as "pure" beings corrupted by parents and culture. Many Americans have ceased to believe in human evil. To the extent that our culture remains interested in evil at all, only one question concerns us: Why do bad things happen?

By contrast, Jesus accepts human evil as a fact of life; he maintains a concern about the universal human potential for evil and about the need for forgiveness as a way back to community and life.[1] In the Gospels he addresses the subject of personal evil repeatedly. He uses the word *evil* frequently as well as equivalents like *wicked, sinner,* and *unrighteous.* The word appears seven times in the Sermon on the Mount alone. Given this emphasis, we cannot complete our consideration of Jesus' practical psychology without integrating an understanding of psychological evil into our framework.

To develop an understanding of psychological evil and of Jesus' manner of addressing it, we will begin with his teachings. Jesus assumes evil is a universal human experience. He says to his disciples at the end of a discourse on prayer, "If you then, who are evil, know how to give good things to your children, how much more will the heavenly Father give the Holy Spirit to those who ask him!" (Lk 11:13). Matthew records a similar saying addressed to the crowd during the Sermon on the Mount. Presumably neither the disciples nor the crowd is deserving of particular notoriety in this regard. This understanding of evil as common to all people seems in harmony with Jesus' eager persistence on granting forgiveness of sins.

Insisting that God's ways are not humanity's ways, Jesus particularly resists the challenges of those who might be considered righteous by first-century standards: the scribes and the Pharisees. These were among the most attentive to the Jewish holiness code and, in fact, resisted Jesus' ministry and questioned his authority the most. When they question his right to forgive sins in healing a paralyzed man, Jesus asks, "Why do you think evil in your hearts?" (Mt 9:4). When they credit Jesus' healing of a deaf-mute to Beelzebub, Matthew records Jesus as saying, "You brood of vipers! How can you speak good things, when you are evil?" (Mt 12:34). Having already established the "evil in [their] hearts," he turns conventional wisdom ("good people do good and evil people do evil") against them to show that they also are evil: "The good person out of the good treasure of the heart produces good, and the evil person out of the evil treasure produces evil; for it is out of the abundance of the heart that the mouth speaks" (Lk 6:45). Jesus flatly refuses to let them test him: "Then some of the scribes and Pharisees said to him, 'Teacher, we wish to see a sign from you.' But he answered them, 'An evil and adulterous generation asks for a sign'" (Mt 12:38–39).

Another way in which Jesus refers to evil is to presuppose a personified source of evil. In The Lord's Prayer he includes the petition "rescue us from the evil one" (Mt 6:13b). Regarding simplicity in giving one's word, he says, "Let your word be 'Yes, Yes' or 'No, No'; anything more than this comes from the evil one" (Mt 5:37). Praying for his disciples, he says, "I ask you to protect them from the evil one" (Jn 17:15b).

Perhaps most remarkable are Jesus' instructions about responding to evil: "Blessed are you when people . . . utter all kinds of evil against you falsely" (Mt 5:11); "Do not resist an evildoer" (Mt 5:39); "But I say to you, love your enemies and pray for those who persecute you, so that you may be children of your Father in heaven; for he makes his sun rise on the evil and on the good, and sends rain on the righteous and on the unrighteous" (Mt 5:44–45). Jesus insists that evil is a universal phenomenon and should not be used as a basis for withholding love from other human beings. We will consider this surprising treatment of evil as we seek to understand psychological evil and its defeat in Jesus' framework.

Psychology's silence about evil has troubled me for years. This silence has troubled M. Scott Peck as well. True to his talent for pithy beginnings, Peck titles the introduction to his *People of the Lie: The Hope for Healing Human Evil,* "Handle with Care," and writes, "This is a dangerous book. I have written it because I believe it is needed. I believe its over-all effect will be healing" (1983, 9). Peck is right on two counts: someone needed to address evil from a psychological perspective, and *People of the Lie* is a dangerous book. Beginning with the case of George, who "made a pact with the Devil" in order to gain control over an obsessive-compulsive behavior, Peck describes a series of blood-chilling cases in which people made choices that endangered or injured the well-being of others. When confronted with their behavior, they exhibited appalling blindness about the meaning of their actions. In several cases, he describes behavior characteristic of clinically character-disordered individuals, and labels them as "evil people." In an attempt to draw a clear definition of evil people, he writes:

> If evil people cannot be defined by the illegality of their deeds or the magnitude of their sins, then how are we to define them? The answer is by the consistency of their sins. While usually subtle, their destructiveness is remarkably consistent. This is because those who have "crossed over the line" are characterized by their *absolute* refusal to tolerate the sense of their own sinfulness (ibid., 71).

There is no question that people with character-disordered personalities callously use and abuse others for their own ends,[2] but I am profoundly uncomfortable with labeling them "evil people," particularly in light of Jesus' emphasis both on the universal potential for evil and on God's care for all. Indeed, one could argue that the secular school of Self-Psychology, whose major single mode of operations is empathy in dealing with character-disordered individuals, is more consistent with the attitudes of Jesus in the Gospels than is Peck's.[3]

While I applaud Peck for raising the important issue of psychological evil, I feel that we ourselves are much closer to the "evil people" he describes than we would like to think. Russian author Aleksandr Solzhenitsyn brings this chilling truth closer to home. After detailing his own rise to authority in the army and then relating events leading to his arrest, Solzhenitsyn confronts a horrifying personal reality: he is already one of "them," one of the executioners. Only upon reflection could he see that before his arrest, he had been just as they were:

> So let the reader who expects this book to be a political expose, slam its covers right now.
>
> If only it were so simple! If only there were people somewhere insidiously committing evil deeds, and it were necessary only to separate them from the rest of us and destroy them. But the line dividing good and evil cuts through the heart of every human being. And who is willing to destroy a piece of his heart?
>
> During the life of any heart this line keeps changing place; sometimes it is squeezed one way by exuberant evil and sometimes it shifts to allow enough space for

good to flourish. One and the same human being is, at various ages, under various circumstances, a totally different human being. At times he is close to being a devil, at times to sainthood. But his name doesn't change, and to that name we ascribe the whole lot, good and evil.

Socrates taught us: *Know thyself!*

Confronted with the pit into which we are about to toss those who have done us harm, we halt, stricken dumb: it is after all only because of the way things worked out that they were the executioners and we weren't (1974, 168).

If we cannot point to personality characteristics that make particular people "evil," what does constitute psychological evil? Two Episcopal priests with considerable training in theology and Jungian psychology have written books that approach the subject of psychological evil: Morton Kelsey's *Discernment, A Study in Ecstasy and Evil,* and John A. Sanford's *Evil: The Shadow Side of Reality.* Consistent with what we have seen in Jesus' treatment of the subject, these priests recognize sin and evil as universal. Evil is a potential for any of us. Struggling to understand the locus of evil in human beings, Kelsey draws on the Jungian concepts of personal and collective unconscious by observing that "forgotten personal experiences" and "powerful universal patterns of experience or archetypes" are capable of intervening and controlling our choices, astonishing us, so that we might find ourselves surprised by our own behavior. In aligning his understanding of evil with Jesus' ministry, Kelsey also dares to introduce a suggestion of the actual presence of spiritual powers and the necessity of our dependence on God:

The human will or ego cannot stand against demonic infiltration and possession unless one is endowed by the Spirit of God which protects a person. . . . One reason that Jesus is so hostile to sickness and sin is that they result from domination of the human being by an alien spirit. Jesus' whole being was hostile to this negative reality.

. . . people are not totally responsible for all their evil or their sickness. . . . Everyone is bearing a heavier burden than we realize, for all men and women are struggling, whether they know it or not, against powers of spiritual darkness (1978, 64–65).

It is our blindness to the unconscious powers within, Kelsey writes, that Jung describes as "evil *par excellence*, the primal human sin," the etiology of all human evil.

It is this point that John Sanford addresses in *Evil: The Shadow Side of Reality*. The Shadow, as he calls it, is a universal pattern in the collective unconscious, or archetype, representing rejected and repressed parts of our personality. We have ignored or denied these elements of ourselves in our striving to be our "ego ideal," or the person our conscious selves would wish us to be. Sanford warns, "The Shadow is never more dangerous than when the conscious personality has lost touch with it" (1984, 55). By way of illustration, he cites a case from literature, Robert Louis Stevenson's *The Strange Case of Dr. Jekyll and Mr. Hyde*. In this story, the righteous and upstanding Jekyll discovers a dark and deformed side of himself, Mr. Hyde. By day he meets the world as the good doctor, and by night his activities become increasingly dominated by Mr. Hyde. As Jekyll begins to realize that he can no longer control whether or not he becomes Hyde, he makes a major mistake. He redoubles his efforts, even through the use of religious discipline that is not necessarily faith, to gain control over, or repress, Hyde. In the end, Mr. Hyde completely takes over as the dominant personality.

Only by facing the Shadow, becoming aware of potential evil within ourselves, can we begin to claim victory. "For the most part, it is only when people encounter evil in some form—as pain, loss of meaning, or something that appears to be threatening or destructive to them—that they begin to find their way to consciousness" (ibid., 40).

Sanford addresses American cultural obliviousness of evil by broaching the subject of evil as a universal fact:

. . . if evil is an archetypal power in the human psyche, as our legend suggests, then not even the best possible environments for people to grow up in and live in will keep evil out of the picture. It can even be suggested that incorrigible criminal personalities are a living representation of the archetypal power. Nor can we assume that all evil behavior in mankind would disappear if every child received the right kind of parenting, with plenty of love and affection (ibid., 115).

Ernest Becker adds another dimension to our consideration of evil. His view returns us to our bodies with a resounding thump. Evil, as Becker understands it, occurs because the human condition exists as a constant tension between appetite and ingenuity. Our basic condition is animal, and we exist because we devour other organisms. To illustrate this fact, he proposes that we would be horrified if at the end of our lives we were presented with the living spectacle of what we had consumed. At the same time, we are not animal in that we know that our own end is inevitable. This, in turn, leads to a desperate attempt on the part of our ingenuity to control life and ensure our significance. On the one hand, we are bound to the earth by our need to feed ourselves while on the other hand we desire to transcend the physical necessities of life and control the world around us. In considering "The Basic Dynamic of Human Evil," Becker quotes Otto Rank:

All our human problems, with their intolerable sufferings, arise from man's ceaseless attempts to make this material world into a man-made reality . . . aiming to achieve on earth a "perfection" which is only to be found in the beyond, thereby hopelessly confusing the values of both spheres.

"Rank's words," Becker concludes, "are a complete scientific formula about the cause of evil in human affairs" (1975, 91). It is this desperate, largely unconscious attempt to control life, riddled with shame over our insignificance, that makes us vulnerable to such evils as devoting ourselves to a totalitarian regime or a dictatorial cause. It is not difficult to note the themes we have already encountered: fearful longing for control over others emerging from the child's painful recognition of separateness from mother, paralyzing shame over our insignificance, desperate swings in either-or thinking, struggle against limitation, finitude, and powerlessness.

If psychological evil begins as a semi-conscious attempt to control life, can we recognize it in ourselves and others? A particular example can be helpful here. Let us examine this pattern of controlling behavior in a seventy-two-year-old grandfather I will call Steve.

Steve's middle child, Shelley, a forty-two-year-old divorced mother of a sixteen-year-old daughter, Barbara, moved to a town within easy driving distance of his home. He had been urging the move for a long time, and finally an attractive teaching position had convinced Shelley, who lived alone because Barbara had elected to remain with her father in another state.

The teaching assignment was a good one for Shelley, but because she now lived closer to her father he called several times a week and insisted that she spend certain evenings with them. When Shelley was with her parents, her father dominated the occasion, grilling her about her finances, her job, and Barbara's health and well-being. At the end of the school year, Shelley required minor emergency surgery, and Steve demanded that she move to their home. Wisely, Shelley moved in with her sister instead, but while she was in the hospital, Steve went to his other daughter's home and went through Shelley's belongings, ostensibly to organize them for her.

When Barbara came to live with Shelley for the summer, Steve offered to celebrate her sixteenth birthday by taking them to a guest ranch for a week. Barbara and Shelley agreed when Steve promised them their own cabin.

On the way to the ranch Steve criticized Barbara about her dress, her makeup, her attitude, and her behavior. He told her that if she did not make some significant changes, she would be very lonely because no one would be able to stand her. Shelley's attempts to intervene only enraged him. During the week, Steve arrived at their cabin at ten o'clock every night, demanding to know where Barbara was. By the end of the week everyone was exhausted and Barbara bitterly hated her grandfather. Later in the summer, a favorite aunt and uncle, who had been living next door to Shelley's parents, announced they were moving away. When Shelley inquired about their decision, they told her quietly that Steve was so dominating it was impossible to live in the same town.

The misery that Steve created for his family and for himself is apparent, but psychological evil is not so much the outcome of behavior (whether or not someone is hurt) as it is the controlling behavior itself. The following story illustrates this point.

Patsy called one evening and reported that she had been off work that day and had been crying most of the day. "What's happening inside?" I inquired. Patsy reported that she felt unbearably lonely even though her housemates were in adjoining rooms. "They have each other," she explained. "Even around them, I feel lonely."

Since this was an emergency call, I used crisis techniques to help her establish stability: "How much are you reading their minds, and how much are you projecting your present loneliness way into the future?"

There was a brief pause on the other end of the line before Patsy responded. "I do both those all the time," she observed. "I have been doing them all day."

"You will probably be unable to stop them from happening," I cautioned. "Both those automatic behaviors are attempts to control others, but what happens when you try them is exactly the reverse of your plan. The more you read minds—that is, attempt to control other people by second-guessing them—the more deeply you will feel powerless because you know at a deep level that you can control only yourself. The more you project worry into the future, the more desperate the present situation will seem. Try to stay in the present if you can, and simply observe yourself trying to read your housemates' minds."

When I saw Patsy two days later, she was feeling relatively good. "I can't believe how much better I felt when I was aware of worrying about the future and of trying to read my roommates' minds. But, honestly, I do those things with everybody. I am always trying to figure out what people think."

"Those automatic behaviors are very hard on you. What would it be like for you if you and I examined that massive loneliness together right here?"

"That's scary. I don't know that I can do it. But I want to."

"What is that feeling like for you?"

"Well, scary. Like a deep empty hole, a void."

I sat quietly for a moment before observing, "That must seem frightening." I paused. "If you looked into the hole, what might you notice?"

"You know," Patsy said suddenly, "if it doesn't last forever, it's not so hard to look at it. I mean, if I stay in the present, it doesn't feel so lonely."

Granted, this is an abbreviated version of what happened, and you might well ask me why I cited this story as an example of psychological evil. What is evil about Patsy's psychological functioning? She certainly is not hurting anyone. Indeed you are correct. At most, she only frightens herself and contributes to her own loneliness. So what is it that Patsy has in common with Steve that I am calling the beginnings of psychological evil? Each of them is operating out of a deeply unconscious sense of terror. Essentially each is emotionally a very small child with an appalling sense of imminent abandonment. Each is desperately trying to control the environment to avert impending disaster. Each is a small child on the verge of a temper tantrum with all that implies: that is, they feel that if they do not get exactly what they want right away, their inner organization will unravel and disintegrate. Steve's bullying intensity, which essentially alienates him from human contact, is at base an inner threat of dissolution of self.

There is a difference, however, between Patsy and Steve. Patsy has begun to recognize her own inner terrified unconscious patterns. At this point, Steve's repression is so complete that he would not recognize himself in my description of him. Patsy also has one relationship, with me, in which she feels some trust and which she cannot control. Within the community of our time together she begins to feel the feelings that so terrify her and begins to become aware of her unconscious, spontaneous patterns of manipulation.

Although in Steve's case it is clearer how his unconscious patterns have done harm to his family, how is it that I call this evil? We can certainly see that he is unpleasant, the type of extended family member that people dread having at a reunion, but how does his behavior relate to what we might consider "serious" evil?

Steve's passion to dominate is without self-reflection and permits no external suggestion. In Steve's mind, for example, he tyrannizes his family for their own good; he lacks self-awareness and is unrepentant. Only social and legal restrictions limit his exercise of power. With more resources and fewer inhibitions, he would be an extremely dangerous man.

One significant control on the extent of Steve's evil is that he has limited power. By contrast, Joseph Stalin had immense power and, according to his daughter's account in *Twenty Letters to a Friend,* we can guess that he also had Steve's chronic, anxious, unconscious misery:

> One wouldn't know the house now. My father had it re-built over and over again. Probably he was just unable to find peace of mind, for the same thing happened with all his houses (Alliluyeva 1967, 20).

In another place she writes:

> My father wouldn't tolerate the slightest attempt to change his mind about anybody. Once he had cast out of his heart someone he had known a long time, once he had mentally relegated that someone to the ranks of his enemies, it was impossible to talk to him about that person any more. He was constitutionally incapable of the reversal that would turn a fancied enemy back into a friend (ibid., 59).

Much as Steve did, Stalin sought to dominate his daughter as completely as he could. With greater resources at his disposal, Stalin had his daughter followed by a security guard who reported every behavior. When she was sixteen, he sent her first serious suitor into exile and then to prison. His wife killed herself when their daughter, Svetlana, was six, a fact that Stalin so successfully suppressed that Svetlana learned the truth ten years later from an American magazine. One wonders how much of the secret police, the blood purges, the wars and oppression of millions were products of Stalin's deep unconscious inner terrors combined with equal terrors of his conspirators. One comes with renewed appreciation for the framers of the United States Constitution, whose respect for evil led them to build a government on limited power.

In Steve, and presumably in Stalin, we can observe the kind of insensitive obliviousness of Scott Peck's "evil" people. However, the source of their evil is not their callous indifference, but their unconscious, terrified longing to be in absolute control. What differs between Steve (and to some extent,

Patsy) on the one hand and Stalin on the other is that Stalin was not a solitary figure. Massive destructiveness takes the collaboration of many.

When our own inner terrors and unconscious longings for control become codified into some pattern of good people versus bad people, we are capable of perpetrating immense evil. Some of the greatest horrors of history result from codified, communal human fear. "Fear," writes Kelsey, "is his infernal majesty's most frequently used instrument" (1978, 85).

We can observe in all of these examples the unconsciousness addressed by Kelsey and Sanford. Steve, Patsy, and Stalin are simply unaware of the Shadow side of their personalities. It is profoundly repressed, and in powerful control. When taken alongside what has been said by Becker, with his graphic (and sometimes repulsive) description of the human being as a tug-of-war between appetite and ingenuity, we are able to catch a glimpse of the essence of human evil that operates in the Shadow. Every human being lives with a largely ignored, but appalling, awareness: no matter how clever individuals may be, no matter what we strive to accomplish, no matter how rich or how generous we are, in the end we all die. "Man is cursed with a burden no animal has to bear: he is conscious that his own end is inevitable, that his stomach will die." Becker goes on to tie this knowledge of death to the innate dread of insignificance experienced by each of us:

> What man really fears is not so much extinction, but extinction *with insignificance.* Man wants to know that his life counted, if not for himself, then at least in a larger scheme of things, that it has left a trace, a trace that has meaning (1975, 3–4).

Powered by a denial of death and a dread of insignificance, experienced at some level as a massive void or a great emptiness, human beings strive for some manner of feeling safe. These primal feelings threaten the psyche with abandonment and obliteration, and an individual begins to engage in clinging and controlling behaviors. It is not hard to recognize the behavior in a very small child, who clings and demands with a sense of panic. We recognize as well the unmodulated feelings of such a child. No control is ever enough; the clinging psyche never feels safe.

The intense power of these feelings becomes increasingly dangerous because the feelings are unconscious. Was the gothic horror of Hitler's Germany essentially that isolated man's frantic attempt to feel safe? Has the United States' fear of communism and our engagement in the arms race been fueled by corporate terror and emptiness, the longing to be safe that is never and can never be satisfied? Is the institutionalized evil of racism that leads to lynchings and apartheid at base an unconscious corporate longing to be safe, to be in control? Instead of finding evil, as Jesus suggests, in ourselves and in our own terrified longing to be in control of the universe, it is easier to find an "all-bad" scapegoat like a racial or religious group or a particular dictator in the world order. We recognize evil in other people. Solzhenitsyn's icy wisdom in stating that we all hold a potential for evil is harder to face.

Since unconsciousness appears to be such a key element in the advancement of psychological evil, it is troubling to think that in the United States people have nearly ceased to believe in psychological evil. This cultural dilemma was illustrated in a recent article in *Time* magazine, "Evil, Does It Exist—or Do Bad Things Just Happen?" The pictorial essay touched upon a little of everything: part of Frederick Buechner's definition of evil from *Wishful Thinking,* references to Satan in *Paradise Lost, The Book of Job,* and *Moby Dick,* and quotes about evil from famous people. The writer had researched his topic. Its pictures included a classic image of Hitler saluting superimposed over inmates from the death camp at Dachau, a hospital photo of a father embracing his AIDS-afflicted son, and a news shot of the bloated bodies of cattle and human beings that died in Bangladesh's 1991 cyclone. It was an ambitious article, which concluded with a philosophical question, "Does good depend on evil?" (Morrow 1991).

The article made me think that the author, like many citizens of the United States since World War II, had not thought much about evil beyond that which is exemplified in the Joseph Stalins and Adolf Hitlers. I finished it feeling fragmented and dissatisfied. The framers of the Constitution believed, much like Solzhenitsyn, in the universal human potential for evil, and consequently limited the power of any particular individual or group. What will be the consequence if and when citizens of the United States have no philosophical understanding of human evil?

There is probably no place that the absence of a philosophical understanding of evil is more apparent than in the American menu for childraising. Children are understood to be entirely good, victims of cruel, or at best, clumsy parenting. One consequence of this view is a radical undermining of parental authority. Anything wrong with a child is understood to be the parents' fault. I am reminded of the child emperor in the film, *The Last Emperor*, who announced to his brother that whenever he did anything "naughty," someone else was punished for it.

An additional consequence is that adulthood with its demands and duties comes to these youngsters as a shock. Unlike very poor cultures where families count on their children's work for survival and much is demanded of adolescents, we accept as culturally and age-appropriate that children and teens do little to help their families. Our culturally accepted leisure status for American adolescents can provide an oasis in which they achieve skills and education for a complex adult life. But it also may send a sadly accurate message that they are not very useful, that they make no significant contribution. Raised in comfortable circumstances with little appreciation for their own potential for evil or for the need to work hard to survive in the world, teens face the transition into adult life with tremendous apprehension and rage. "S——t happens, and then you die," as one high school saying has put it. Comfortable children at this transition struggle against commitments. Nothing is quite good enough. They may resist adulthood by developing an emotional illness. Like Steve and Patsy, they fall back on unconscious primitive bids for control, essentially a demand to remain a child. The anorexic teen, for example, loses her menstrual period and looks like a prepubescent child. If her family is not already deeply involved, her crisis terrifies them into becoming overinvolved. She places herself in a position that demands constant care, a return to infancy. As we saw with Stalin and Hitler, once the unconscious panicky demand for control, the reptile brain, is in place, no control is ever enough. Unless she is forced to eat, an anorexic youngster, in search of perfect control, will starve herself to death.

Evil is universal, Jesus reminds us, and we are in grave danger when we fail to take that fact seriously. Psychological evil is the deeply hidden longing in each human being to be in absolute control. It presents itself to us at a conscious level quite sensibly as wanting to be safe. But the primitive terror and rage of a small child fuels it. Theologically, it is our battle against our finitude, our longing to be "like God, knowing good and evil," as the story of Adam and Eve's temptation in Eden (Gn 3) illustrates. While it remains unconscious, we are likely to engage in a variety of controlling behaviors. Like Steve, we may attempt to force others to do as we wish. Like Patsy, we may try to read others' minds and change our actions accordingly. Our quest for absolute security and control often becomes institutionalized in holiness codes or perfect belief systems: "People who believe or act as I do are good; everyone else is evil." At the same time, however, these unconscious attempts to achieve security leave us vulnerable to "the Accuser" or "the Enemy" who drives us without mercy: We are perfect or we are nothing; we are loved by all or we are abandoned. It is to this terrible dilemma that the Incarnation speaks. Before I elaborate, let me illustrate how the quest for control through attempting to be perfect operates by using the following personal story.

I met Valerie when she was a senior at the University of California at Berkeley, an honor student in accounting. An established firm had courted and hired her at the end of her junior year. She reported having trouble finishing her final semester; she was suffering from intense nightmares. A member of a group of devotees to recent inspired writings, *The Urnasha Book*, referred her to me because she wanted someone who would be sympathetic to a religious orientation. No mention of faith was made for some time, except reference to a church in their farming community that she and her mother had attended for respite from family violence. Valerie's childhood was replete with incidents of her father's cruel teasing and violent punishment. She recited a litany of events that occurred at the ages of four, five, six, eight. At eleven he had promised her a horse if she received excellent grades, but when she achieved them he mocked her foolishness for believing he would honor the agreement.

Eventually her mother's fragile self-esteem disintegrated, and she was hospitalized on several occasions. Her parents divorced, and Valerie's maternal grandmother moved in with her mother, her brother, and herself. Gradually, Valerie accepted many caretaking roles for her physically fragile grandmother and her psychologically distressed mother. When her estranged father began prowling around the outside of the house with a shotgun, she was unable to gain protection from the small town police force, most of them her father's friends.

"It was so wrong, so wrong. It was just so unfair and so wrong," Valerie protested in my office. "I was such a good kid, and when I tried to tell anyone, they would just say, 'What's so bad about that? It's just normal.' Nanny [her father's mother] would tell me to stop being such a crybaby."

School was also a problem for this exceptional child. She excelled in everything, which made her unpopular with the children and a problem for some teachers. More important, she felt odd. There was no one like her and no place to "belong." She vacillated between feeling superior and feeling terrified.

As a client, Valerie was often late. When I commented on this, she was visibly shaken, protesting that she was always late. "Why does that bother people? It's just who I am." In the next few weeks, she canceled or changed appointments, finally forgetting one until the last minute when she called and left a message on my answering machine. The next time I saw her, I could feel the wall between us. She was unable to make eye contact, and protested that she thought she should stop therapy, try something else.

"What's this about?" I asked. "What is going on between us here?"

Finally she started to cry, "I've been bad. I've been late, and I missed an appointment. I should look at you when I talk. It's not safe anymore. Either I am perfect, or I have to run. You see, I have all these rules . . ."

"So this is what you require of yourself? It must be a terrific strain."

We talked for some time about this split—either she was perfect, or she was despicable, unforgivably bad. "Perhaps," I suggested gently, "you need a demotion. It sounds as though you are straining to be God, and that's too much for any of us to handle."

I concluded our session with what she already knew. "I think it's very important for you to continue therapy." We made a next appointment.

Some months later a similar incident occurred with her job, which she was preparing to quit. "Once I've begun to do bad things, I can't go back." She paused. "You know, that's how the church was helpful. Everyone was a sinner. At night you confessed your sins. It was a way back, and I wasn't alone. I miss that. There's too much in Christianity I don't believe, but at least I had a way back."

After the enormity of the evil Valerie has suffered, it felt unbearable to me to recognize evil in her. In truth she accused herself of evil, horribly, and no amount of intervention from me could persuade her otherwise. Gripped with terror, longing for a safe world, and unable to trust, she built rigid rules. She was safe only if she followed them perfectly and could, therefore, retain an arrogant distance from the world. She did not feel she could trust God because God loved everyone, and "what does that mean anyway?"

The Christian tradition of confession of sin offered her "a way back." What does she mean by "a way back"? A way back to or from what? I suggest it offers a way back to human community and a way back into finitude after desperate, panicky attempts to be God in her longing for safety. The acknowledgment of sin—that is, the recognition of evil in human life, including herself—was a tremendous relief after the horror of repeated denial and fearful insecurity with which she grew up.

It is Valerie's dilemma and our own to which the Incarnation speaks. Jesus, as God become human, embraces finitude without control, without resistance, and without separation from God. In the temptation stories he refuses to be anything but human empowered by God. Throughout his life, he speaks honestly about the universal human potential for evil, and with solid integrity he consistently confronts the organized

privilege that would avoid this truth. Through insistent forgiveness he offers us a way back into human community and
new life. He teaches and demonstrates that God does not
keep score, but offers good gifts—sun and rain—to good and
evil alike. He encourages his followers to do the same, thereby acknowledging themselves as true children of God.

Jesus blesses those who have been the victims of evil because of their integrity (Mt 5:11). He admonishes followers not
to resist evil, but to "turn the other cheek," and in the end he
himself does not resist evil. Instead he surrenders (Jn 18:
1–11), placing himself in the hands of those who hate him,
those who live for ultimate safety and guaranteed control. I
consciously choose the word *surrender* to describe Jesus' behavior in John's account of his arrest. As he submits to arrest,
Jesus demonstrates a choice. In choosing radical monotheism,
obedience to the one God, he exposes the idolatry of those
with all the answers. The exposure incurs their terror and
rage. In the end Jesus faces the result of challenging unconscious, codified fear: torture and death. He surrenders to the
ultimate lack of control, death. Jesus leads us once again into
a major paradox—this time, life's ultimate paradox: only
through surrender is evil ultimately destroyed. Only through
death is death defeated.

Walter Wink writes:

> Because they could not kill what was alive in [Jesus], the
> cross revealed the impotence of death. Death is the
> Powers' final sanction. Jesus at his crucifixion neither
> fights the darkness nor flees under cover of it, but goes
> with it, goes into it. Jesus entered the darkness, freely,
> voluntarily. The darkness in not dispelled or illuminated.
> It remains vast, untamed, void. But he somehow encom-
> passes it. It becomes the darkness of God. It is now pos-
> sible to enter any darkness and trust God to wrest from it
> meaning, coherence, resurrection (1994, 12).

The Significance of Scars

A t a church retreat day one December, the leader asked us
to draw a timeline of our lives, marking on it important
events, particularly an earliest memory. Following this we
were to make a second line, running parallel, indicating high
and low points over our lifetimes. We were asked to note at
which points our faith seemed strongest and, this completed,
to share with one other person what we had discovered. To
our surprise, most of us found the earliest memory represented an incident that shaped our lives. In some cases it was
perceived as a sort of trauma, even a scar. My partner, a peace
activist in our church, remembered being wakened by his
mother to view the first long distance telecast: an atomic bomb
test in the desert. My own memory at about two-and-a-half involved telling an adult guest that my birthday was in "Knocked
over" (October). She and my mother laughed good-naturedly,
as people do with small children, and corrected my pronuncia-
tion, but I felt humiliated and stupid. It was an experience that
would be repeated variously during my dyslexic childhood in
those days when so little was known about the subject. This
early memory, like my partner's, significantly influenced my
life: in this case, my choice to pursue doctoral studies.

We participants in the December retreat day made two
more discoveries. Our particular low points tended to be followed by high points, and the low points tended to have a
positive influence on the depth of our faith. I am reminded of

a gospel-like image used by a masters candidate from New College Berkeley while sharing her own suffering with me over coffee: "God doesn't make bad things happen," she mused. "It's like when you wring out a towel. God wrings every drop of good possible from a terrible situation."[1]

Evil is inevitable and unavoidable. Encounters with it mark our lives and in some ways shape our personalities and our choices. The evil we encounter is not only outside us; it is also within. Evil, as we have seen in chapter 9, emerges from an unconscious resistance to our inescapable vulnerability as human beings. It results in a bid for power to be totally in control of our environment, a forlorn effort to feel safe. As it is unconscious, it is also universal. It is within us and within our friends and loved ones as well as in those we do not like. Blindly driven by this phenomenon, we are likely to do some damage as well as to make life miserable for ourselves through splitting into either-or thinking: "either I am perfect, or I am nothing; either I am loved by all, or I am abandoned." And yet in spite of everything, God also wrings good out of it. It may be that our encounters with evil that scar us also call us into sensitivity and ministry. Some would argue that it is only our suffering that draws us into our humanity. As one pastor put it, "Never trust a person who doesn't limp."

Contrary to the enthusiastic urgings of popular culture, there is no anxiety-free "healed" life through which we may move with untroubled "self-esteem." This is true not only for ourselves, but for our children as well. There is no way to raise a child free from anxiety with an untarnished self-image. The universal fact of suffering in human beings recalls for us yet again Jesus' enthusiastic pronouncements of forgiveness. Jesus seemed to understand how terrible it is to be caught in this unconscious evil. Jesus' approach to evil as we encounter it in other human beings suggests living as if the kingdom of God had arrived: "But I say to you, Do not resist an evildoer. But if anyone strikes you on the right cheek, turn the other also." (Mt 5:39). On a psychological level this advice has profound significance.

Evil in other human beings and in ourselves is not the only danger that we face. This frightening world is clearly beyond our control. Human evil contributes to massive suffering through such instances as prejudice, war, and cruelty, but our lives are touched and shaped by other forces as well: congenital defects, illnesses, and forces of nature. For example, I began working on this chapter in my home in Berkeley, California, on an unseasonably hot and windy October afternoon, an afternoon that produced a firestorm that destroyed three thousand homes in the Oakland-Berkeley hills surrounding our church. This disaster came two years after northern California's 7.1 Loma-Prieta earthquake. Recurring forces of destruction, natural and human, are part of our reality, and no matter how comfortably we live, no matter how strongly we engage in denial, we are subconsciously aware of this. No matter how carefully we nurture and support our children in their vulnerable years, they are also aware of it. We and our children are not only aware of our own vulnerability, but also that of others. In Robert Coles's study of children of the very rich, those who have been carefully sheltered from any suffering that money can prevent, he found that most of these children worried about and prayed for workers in mines their families owned, the migrant workers on the family lands, and the children integrating public schools they would never see. They were aware that cooks and maids working in their homes often spent more time with them than with their own children and observed that such a fact must make them and their children sad (1977). Children of parents with fewer material resources may fare better because they are not kept from reality as successfully. One Mississippi mother of five explained how she coped with her children's early confrontation with racism:

> When they ask all the questions, they ask about their color, too . . . I never have known what to say, except that the Lord likes everyone because He makes everyone, and nothing is so good it can satisfy Him completely, so He made many kinds of people, and they're all equal before Him. Well, that doesn't always satisfy them; not completely it doesn't. So I have to go on. I tell them that no matter what it's like around us, it may make us feel bad, but it's not the whole picture, because we don't make ourselves. It's up to God, and He can have an idea that will fool us all . . . It's the favorite child sometimes who you make sure you don't spoil (Coles 1967, 63–64).

From the vulnerability of being in a racial minority, this mother knows clearly what "privileged ones" are tempted to forget: we can never completely protect our children from the innate knowledge that we are vulnerable and we are finite. Such efforts only encourage children to repress all awareness and engage in denial. Christians sometimes engage in a kind of denial we recognize in the biblical account of Job's friends who visited him in his suffering: "If we really love God, have faith, or believe the right things, then God will protect us from anything bad happening." Following this logic, if something bad does happen to us, then we are not only to blame, but we are exposed to our community as having insufficient faith. This, of course, is not faith, but one more attempt to be ultimately in control.

Whether or not we are affected directly by immense traumas like fires and earthquakes, evil is universal and inescapable. It does and will affect our lives at many points. What happens to us then when trauma hits, especially early in life? I suggest that we are scarred by our encounters with evil, and these scars have a significant influence on how we live our lives.

I am well aware that these statements run counter to much that has been directly stated or implied in popular culture. A great deal of self-help literature is given to psychological "healing" that will make us "normal." Normal is not exactly defined, but implies self-confidence and self-reliance. If I am sufficiently "healed," mostly of traumas that occurred in my childhood, the reasoning goes, then I will feel good about myself most of the time and handle life with expedience and aplomb. In fact, such reasoning suggests, I will be able to achieve the cultural ideals for my age and sex: I can become competent, attractive, articulate, and knowledgeable. Unfortunately, the emphasis on "normal" becomes translated into "life shouldn't be hard," a statement I hear often in working with clients as a counselor. The logic runs like this: I should be able to achieve the self-esteem I want, the competence and career I want, the marriage or relationship I want, and not have to work too hard at it. If I suffer a significant loss through death of a loved one, divorce, or loss of a job, I should be able to be healed and return to "normal." This glib description of hope for healing, which I hear often from clients, would not be shared by most clinicians who know that it is a lengthy process to reverse psychological patterns that have been set in place by trauma. On the contrary, significant trauma, particularly early trauma, affects us deeply, touching us in ways that may remain with us for our lifetimes. To illustrate this point, consider the following story.

Teri first sought my help in her early thirties when she found herself experiencing such extreme anxiety that she was unable to pursue a career in music as she had hoped. My clinical history in working with Teri includes four years of twice-monthly sessions, a modest clinical arrangement meant to accommodate Teri's schedule and budget, followed by a two-year break, and then an additional period of a year after her father's death, followed by a two-year break. At this writing, I am again working with Teri, now 44, in a second year of twice-monthly sessions.

Teri was born to a Bay Area family. Her mother was a homemaker, and her father taught at a university. One summer Saturday morning when she was three, she had begged her father to take her with him on an errand to the hardware store. But he was in a hurry that morning and did not want to be slowed down by a three-year-old, so he refused. He instructed his daughter to play in the back yard with her five-year-old brother, Danny. Their mother, pregnant and with some fear of losing the baby, had to lie down and was not watching the children. That morning the fire department arrived to burn off a vacant lot across the street from their house, and Teri and Danny slipped out of the yard in the company of other neighborhood children to watch with fascination. After the fire department left and the neighborhood children began to disperse, Teri, barefoot, followed Danny into the field to explore. She accidentally stepped into an area of hot coals, but when she tried to get away, her tee-shirt got caught on the barbed wire. Danny, who was wearing shoes, ran to her assistance, but his five-year-old hands could not free the cloth. He ran screaming to their mother, but was so hysterical he could not tell his mother what had happened. Eventually two junior high school boys heard Teri screaming, ran to the lot, freed the little girl, and carried her home. When the horrified mother received her little girl, the child's feet were smoldering with third degree burns. As her mother called for an ambulance, Teri said stoically, "Mommy, I burned my feet." In her shock and confusion Teri's mother left her five-year-old son home alone to give the news to his father. Teri's father and brother came to the hospital later and remained with her until the hospital staff told them to leave. Her father left reluctantly and to his death remembered hearing his daughter's repeated panicky plea, "Daddy, don't leave me," follow him down the stairs and out into the parking lot. When he repeated the story to Teri in her mid-thirties, he wept.

Unknown to the rest of the family, Danny, devastated that he had not been able to protect his little sister, guiltily gathered the bits of charred flesh scattered throughout the house and buried them with a stick cross in his best friend's yard. He was not the only burdened party. Teri's father was shattered because he had not taken his daughter with him to the store, and her mother was stunned that she had not more carefully supervised the children in the yard. Teri, employing the magical thinking of a three-year-old, interpreted the pain of the accident and her father's leaving her in the hospital as just punishment for some terrible crime she had committed. She became depressed and stopped eating; the hospital staff was forced to send her home for fear she would die. Returning home to her traumatized family, Teri absorbed the guilt and anger like a dry sponge. At thirty-five, recounting the story through flowing tears, Teri begged, "I didn't do something terribly wrong, did I?" And even through my own tears, I knew there was nothing I could do to reassure her or to obliterate her magical sense of responsibility. Teri, through the omnipotent imagination of a child, had become "like God." The only alternative would have been for her to understand fully the extent of her vulnerability and powerlessness in the situation. She was absolutely unable to endure that knowledge.

This is the story that shapes Teri's life; it is an indelible scar. Like the fire that ripped through the Oakland-Berkeley hills and the earthquake that collapsed a freeway, the magnitude of such tragedy appalls us. We are speechless before it. It leaves us face-to-face with the sure knowledge that something like this could just as easily have occurred in our own families. But this knowledge is unbearable and engenders anger. In the face of such tragedy, it is tempting to hide our knowledge of vulnerability in righteous indignation: "This shouldn't have happened. Someone is to blame." One form of denial involves blaming the victims: one grocery clerk reflecting on the firestorm proclaimed, "Those people should have cut back the shrubbery around their homes." Certainly Teri's family engaged in "this-shouldn't-have-happened" thinking, individually flagellating themselves in desperate, secret isolation, individually confronting their failure to assume effectively the role of ever-protective God figure. Is this the suffering Jesus discerned in his eager offering of forgiveness? Would he not wish to gather this devastated family to him as "a hen gathers her chicks"? But, like Jerusalem of old, the family was so caught in their suffering that they could not have heard the call.

Sometimes Christians confronted with tragedy of this magnitude retreat into denial: "God wouldn't have let this happen to us. Why did he let it happen to them?" Like Job's comforters who were forced by his tragedy to face their own vulnerability,[2] Christian friends might conclude that this family must have had a secret moral failing or some collapse in their faith. Or perhaps God is the one seen as responsible: "It's God's will."[3] These unanswerable assumptions emanate from the depth of our fear of finitude.

What does the New Testament say about appalling tragedy? Teri lives with permanently damaged feet that the best of medical knowledge has not been able to heal. She lives with a psychological scar that she has worked through on many levels for eleven years. But Teri's is only one of many stories of tragedy that clinicians hear daily. One person lost her mother to cancer at three years old and is so consumed with rage at her stepmother for daring to marry her father that she fears she has been possessed by the devil. Another person's atomic scientist father sexually molested him during periods of drunkenness over several years. A third whose immigrant parents routinely dropped her off at a local convent for preschool childcare suffers from a panicky fear of abandonment. In every case we might be tempted to rage, "This should not have happened. Someone is to blame. Perhaps God. At least, God should have stopped it."

At least in the culture of the United States there is a sense that life ought not to be so cruel. We strive to protect our children and ourselves, to give them comfort and education, to build their self-esteem. Under ordinary circumstances, the reasoning goes, people "should" grow up to be successful and confident. This cultural rendering of narcissistic entitlement was demonstrated for me at the local swimming pool by a twenty-three-year-old expert swimmer discussing the firestorm with the pool manager. "As if we needed another tragedy," she complained loudly across two swim lanes as she worked out on a kick board. "Kids are having a hell of a time and the adults. . . ." The gray-haired manager cut her off. "Welcome to life," he shouted back, his voice friendly, but his message pointed. "It's called reality."

Practicing Christians, enculturated as Americans, have their own version of narcissistic entitlement: God should protect and rescue us, make my endeavors prosper, and protect my self-esteem. If these things fail, perhaps there is something wrong with my faith. Nevertheless the vocabulary is very similar: "This shouldn't have happened" or "Why did this happen to me?" or even, as Teri thought, "God must be punishing me for something. I don't get it." These responses to life are a long way from Jesus' admonition, "Do not resist evildoers."

If our resistance when bad things happen arises from a deep sense of fear possibly combined with some magical reasoning that we ought to have prevented it, Jesus' model of nonresistance demonstrates integrity and ironic personal power. In fact, as we observe his enactment of nonresistance, we approach the profound mysteries at the heart of Christian faith. Nonresistance as integrity and power is vividly demonstrated in gospel accounts of Jesus' arrest at Gethsemane, his trial, and crucifixion.

All four Gospels culminate in the passion narrative and the crucifixion with abundant foreshadowing as if the horrific nature of these events demands interpretation. Matthew, speaking to a Jewish audience, carefully demonstrates Jesus' life and death as fulfilling the Messianic promises of the Old Testament. The events from Jesus' prayer vigil in Gethsemane to his crucifixion enact submission to God, radical monotheism. This submission paradoxically combines power and powerlessness. Joel Green notes, "In this context Jesus' authority as God's Son occupies center stage, but he does not exercise this power as a means of escape" (1992, 156). In keeping with what we have observed in the temptation story and through-out his ministry, Jesus refuses to move beyond the limits of finitude. Jesus, the Incarnation, invites us into blessed human-ness, obedient to and empowered by God. Jesus does not re-sist the evildoers at his arrest, and the power of his integrity dominates the story:

> Now the betrayer had given them a sign, saying, "The one I will kiss is the man; arrest him." At once he came to Jesus and said, "Greetings, Rabbi!" and kissed him. Jesus said to him, "Friend, do what you are here to do." Then they came and laid hands on Jesus and arrested him. Suddenly, one of those with Jesus put his hand on his sword, drew it, and struck the slave of the high priest, cutting off his ear. Then Jesus said to him, "Put your sword back into its place; for all who take the sword will perish by the sword. Do you think that I can-not appeal to my Father, and he will send me more than twelve legions of angels? But how then would the scrip-tures be fulfilled, which say it must happen in this way?" At that hour Jesus said to the crowds, "Have you come out with swords and clubs to arrest me as though I were a bandit? Day after day I sat in the temple teaching, and you did not arrest me. But all this has taken place, so that the scriptures of the prophets may be fulfilled." Then the disciples deserted him and fled (Mt 26:48–56).

We must take seriously Jesus' full humanity in this remark-able account, or we diminish its power and its challenge to our own lives. Jesus' obedience is based, like ours, on searching prayerful understanding of God's demanding love in its plan for the world. His foreknowledge is no more than ours. The only power he employs is human power: integrity and faith. Here, as in the temptation story, he refuses to desert the terri-fying realm of finitude for the safety of divinity. God's plans for a redeemed world lie embedded in the human endeavor.

Remarkably, Jesus calls his betrayer "friend," thereby in-cluding one even in this setting who has made himself not just an outcast but an enemy. Second, refusing to resist the evil of the arrest himself, he also stops his disciple's attempt to fight. Third, in the face of overwhelming military might, he asks a rhetorical question: "Have you come out with swords and clubs to arrest me as though I were a bandit? Day after day I sat in the temple teaching, and you did not arrest me" (Mt 26:55). In that setting it is a powerless question; but no reader can miss its power.

"Do not resist an evildoer," Jesus counsels his disciples, and in his arrest and trial, he does not resist. Green writes that "Jesus . . . is convinced that suffering lies at the heart of his mission as Christ, Son of God, and even extends this definition to his view of discipleship" (ibid.). Jesus' suffering reconciles humanity to God. Our suffering too can be appropriated by God for healing the world.

During much of his trial, Jesus remains silent. Herman Waetjen in his book *A Reordering of Power* notes that Jesus' silent nonresistance places him outside the cycle of power and retaliation and enables continued nonjudgmental solidarity with all human beings and with God. Stepping outside the cycle of retaliation in solidarity and acceptance even with our enemies takes from our hands once and for all the attempted power seized in the Fall: to be "like God knowing good and evil" (Gn 3). But Jesus' integrity, his refusal to retaliate, opens a door for God not only to wring good from bad, but to enact the mystery of the cross. Waetjen writes:

> Atonement is effected, and God and human beings are reconciled to each other. For in his experience of divine abandonment Jesus also refuses to renounce or surrender his solidarity with God. Even in his desolation he still cries, "*My* God, *my* God." Rejected and smitten by both God and humankind, he nevertheless cleaves to both as he absorbs their enmity. Consequently he becomes the bridge that unites them, the bridge that spans the nothingness of death and links human beings once more to the source of life and possibility (1989, 236).

Jesus cancels the power of enmity between God and humanity for all time, restoring human beings as heirs of the kingdom, opening once again the source of life and possibility.

What does this have to say to someone like Teri, whose horrifying early trauma has left an indelible scar on both her body and her psyche, scars that never let her forget that early terror and her remaining vague sense of guilt and vulnerability? Can meaning be wrung out of Teri's suffering as well? Is not Teri's accident, like the Oakland-Berkeley fire, just a terrible senseless tragedy that should never have happened? Will those who lost homes and in some cases everything but their lives as well as those who avoided the fire not live with an ongoing sense of horror? Is it not better when we can live a protected life and keep such horrors of the world away from the eyes of our children? What does the gospel have to say about scars?

There is no question that many of us use every means at our disposal to protect our children and prevent tragedies from happening, but as Robert Coles discovered in his study of children of privilege, even the most careful planning cannot make a system of denial complete. And those less protected may demonstrate remarkable resilience. Ironically, were we in the United States to succeed perfectly in our cultural design—each generation becoming reliably more comfortable and competent than its predecessor—we would have nothing to say to the world. There would be nothing in our lives to draw us into compassionate understanding of humanity in any loving and appreciative way. It is our scars that make us credible, and it is our scars that make us sensitive. It was Jesus' scars, as well, that made him credible in his own day as well as among suffering people of the world in our day. In resurrection accounts when Jesus encountered doubting and troubled followers, he established his identity not by brilliant discussion nor by miracles, but by his scars. Indeed for Thomas, it was Jesus' scars that made him credible. John's Gospel relates this story:

> But Thomas . . . was not with them when Jesus came . . . he said to them, "Unless I see the mark of the nails in his hands, and put my finger in the mark of the nails in his hands, and put my hand in his side, I will not believe."
>
> A week later . . . Jesus came and stood among them and said, "Peace be with you." Then he said to Thomas, "Put your finger here and see my hands. Reach out your hand and put it in my side. Do not doubt but believe." (Jn 20:24, 25b, 26a, c, 27)

How exactly then do our scars make us credible and how do our encounters with trauma draw us into compassionate and involved living? Probably the most common example is what happens to our understanding of parents after we have children. There is a story about a young doctor who lectured at Parent-Teacher Associations on "Ten Requisites for Good Parenting." After the birth of his first child, he changed the lecture to "Ten Ideas for Parenting." After the birth of his second child, he changed the title again, "Ten Suggestions for Parenting." After the birth of a third child, he stopped lecturing altogether.

This anecdote is probably universally verified. In a parent communication group I taught for mothers, most participants had been teachers, nurses, or church school workers before having their own children. As we shared our personal transformations in dealing with parenting, we laughed a lot. As one woman put it, "Parenting is so constant. It's twenty-four hours a day, day after day, week after week. You can't escape from it."

But I think we also know that something deepening can happen to us when we go through experiences we ordinarily would have avoided at all costs. Something in us changes permanently. People who have endured, survived, and demonstrated character attract us. Victor Frankl emerged from his death camp experience with an understanding of a psychology of meaning. Anna Ornstein, another Auschwitz survivor, became a major contributor to Self-Psychology, fine tuning her sensitive clinical empathy. Ben Weir, after sixteen months as a hostage held in Lebanon, was elected as head of the Presbyterian Church of the United States. We believed he had something to say to us. In Japan, the disfigured survivors of Hiroshima became leaders of the peace movement. In the aftermath of the Oakland-Berkeley firestorm, the survivors themselves, as they recovered within our church community, healed the rest of us who were not directly affected. Each of these people has something to say to us; their scars make them credible.

But closer to home, most of us know those whose lives have been shaped by moments they would have longed to avoid. Nina, whom I knew four years, taught me to see the little blessings in life through her dying from cancer. In the

Twelve Step programs, people find help from others who like themselves have suffered. Their scars make them credible. It is perhaps not the United States, efficient and privileged, that will ultimately offer hope to the world, but rather India, Brazil, and Kenya.

How about Teri, with her crippled feet and frightened spirit? How could God wring good out of the immense tragedy of that summer morning? Perhaps the answer is in the life she has lived. At this point she has not developed a career in music. She holds an administrative assistant's position where she supervises two other employees and trains student interns. She has a remarkable ability to maintain close, loving relationships with friends and colleagues. She is a mood-setter in her office. Her determination to understand and overcome the impact of tragedy upon her has brought increasing intimacy and nurture to her family. She has facilitated conversation about her accident with each member of the family, eliciting tears and stories, and healing of the guilty secret. In addition to her considerable warmth, she is tough enough to discipline an employee or confront a member of the family on manipulative behavior. The condition of her feet significantly limits athletic activity, though she does some bicycling and hiking. The boldness that initially took her onto the vacant lot remains part of her life as well: she is a pilot.

In her "ministry" to her family, Teri's scars made her credible. She was the only one who could raise the issues and draw the family out of guilty isolation into unusual family intimacy. Her determination to face the issues made her a healer. Teri has yet one more task in her encounter with evil: she must face the utter powerlessness she experienced as a child.

One area of Teri's life that has not worked well is her relationship with men. In our work together we unearthed a fantasy that she would only be safe if she had a man who would take care of her, offer her everything and yield to all her demands. It is not hard to recognize the familiar infant fantasy of symbiotic union with mother, which we explored in chapter 3. Teri's search for this perfect man had a frantic quality to it. During the first break in our working relationship, Teri divorced her husband when he declined an offer from both sets of parents that would have enabled them to build a house and refused to consider having a baby. Later when her father died, Teri experienced panic attacks that caused her difficulty in breathing. Subsequently, she had a series of romantic relationships. In each she exhibited the excellent interpersonal skills that served her so well at work and with her family, but underneath there remained a brittle quality that set up in her waves of panic. "I just don't feel loved. I don't feel loved," she complained to her former husband who remained a very close friend. "Teri, honey," he argued, "This doesn't make sense. Your brothers love you, I love you, your friends love you. What more do you want?" Although Teri could understand it logically, she was unable to prevent the feelings.

Working carefully together we fleshed out the pattern. When she was romantically involved with a man, she became attached in a clingy way. If he were not immediately available to her, she experienced waves of panic, imagined all sorts of things that might have happened to him, or other women he might prefer to be with. She was experiencing what a small child feels when its mother leaves the room, a terrible panic that she may never return. The panic was like being on the verge of a temper tantrum with all that entails for a small child: to some degree Teri felt that if she did not immediately have access to the person, she would disintegrate. The terror was intense and very real. "This little child inside me," Teri said, " believes that if I have total control of some man, then I will be safe!" Her forehead wrinkled with exasperation, "That's crazy! I make a perfectly good living. I'm more stable and more solvent than most men I know. What is this?"

"Gently, gently," I cautioned. "Just allow yourself to recognize what is happening when you notice you feel stress. That terrible fear of being hurt, of having needed someone to protect you. You have gotten caught in the magical thinking of the little child: if I can merge with someone stronger, then I will be safe."

As Teri has caught herself in the panic and recognized the pattern as it has happened, she has experienced considerable relief. "You have gone through a demotion," I suggested. "You no longer have imaginary, godlike magical control. You're just another vulnerable human being like the rest of us."

"Boy!" Teri exclaimed with her customary animation. "It sure feels good!"

Ironically, Teri's relief came as a direct result of her willingness to stop resisting evil. If we understand "evil" in a psychological sense as deep vulnerable feelings that confront us with our finitude—powerlessness, abandonment, and emptiness— we recognize that these had driven Teri most of her life. All her efforts to escape, to be safe, deepened her fear. Once Teri understood the pattern, she no longer resisted. She relinquished her panicky efforts to achieve control and found her fear abating. The Incarnation invites us into finitude where blessing awaits us.

Life jolts and wounds us, and we carry the scars, the results of those wounds, throughout our lives. Some of us have grown up in a family plagued with alcoholism. Others have struggled with poverty. Some have suffered from racism. Others have endured a disability, a serious illness, or a deformity. Very often it is by these experiences that we identify ourselves and by them we set the course of our lives.

From the perspective of popular culture, this is tragic: we will never really be "whole." Life will never be pain free. From a Christian perspective, these scars mark the beginning of faith, compassion, and ministry. Frederick Buechner writes, "Christianity . . . ultimately offers no theoretical solution at all [as an explanation for suffering]. It merely points to the cross and says that, practically speaking, there is no evil so dark and so obscene—not even this—but God can turn it to good" (1973, 24). Jesus' words of comfort to our world continue to ring true not because God rescued him, but because he moved with integrity into the heart of suffering, rejection, and death. And out of this, the terrible power of God brought everlasting victory.

It is significant that the risen Christ identified himself to troubled and doubting followers not by brilliant persuasion nor by miracles, but by his scars. It was his suffering, transformed by God, that made him credible. Likewise we, too, need not despair because of the scars that identify us. It is precisely these scars that God transforms into ultimate good for ourselves and compassionate ministry to others.

When the worst that life might deal us can be so transformed, we encounter a "resurrection psychology." Our confidence lies not in preventing anything bad from happening to us, nor in seeking perfect healing of our psychological wounds, but rather our confidence lies in the transforming power of God promised us through the Resurrection of Jesus Christ.

Notes

Foreword

1. This is true in spite of many claims to the contrary in recent "lives of Jesus" issued by major, "secular" publishing houses; see the critical comments in Green 1993.

2. I use *habitus* in the sense employed by Pierre Bourdieu (1991).

Chapter 1

1. Throughout this chapter I stress that the forgiveness of God, which Jesus enthusiastically offered and taught, precedes repentance. Repentance connects us with forgiveness. I am *not* suggesting, however, that human beings should will to adopt this extravagant forgiveness as a model for their own behavior. Many churches, for example, have prematurely urged rape and sexual abuse victims to forgive their abusers. I subscribe to Marie Fortune's assertion that forgiveness flows from one who has power to one who does not have power; therefore abuse victims are not in a position to offer forgiveness. Ironically, continued abuse and its secret imply a "forgiveness" that interferes with the abuser's ability to face his guilt. See Fortune 1989.

2. Jesus' choice to be inclusive is remarkably radical since the first-century Mediterranean world was an *agonistic* culture, from the Greek word *agon* meaning a contest between equals. Bruce Malina explains: "Now in the first-century Mediterranean world, every social interaction that takes place outside one's family or outside one's circle of friends is perceived as a challenge to honor, a mutual attempt to acquire honor from one's social equal. . . . Since honor and reputation, like all goods in life, are limited, then every social interaction of this type comes to be perceived

as an affair of honor, a contest or game of honor, in which play-
ers are faced with wins, ties, and losses" (1981, 32–33).

3. Table fellowship is a mark of extreme intimacy among equals in
the honor- and shame-based culture of Jesus' world. It is generally
reserved for family and equals. Joel Green addresses this issue in
discussing Jesus' choice to eat with tax collectors: "Refusal to
share a meal with another serves an important function in this and
other cultural contexts: It signifies social ostracism, the designation
of someone as excluded from an identified group. In this case,
Jesus' host and fellow guests were regarded as persons of lower
status to be avoided, especially at table" (1984, 18).

4. I owe to the late Elizabeth Hough, then a student at New College
for Advanced Christian Studies, Berkeley, Calif., the suggestion
that the woman in John 8:1–11 is a sexual abuse victim and that
Jesus gave her the ability to say no.

5. Intense family distress does not guarantee failure of children. The
story of resilient children is understudied and has not reached popular literature. One detailed study conducted in Kauai, Hawaii, indicated that inadequate perinatal care alone was less destructive
than is usually assumed (Werner, Bierman, and French 1971).

6. Freud, however, understood shame as an innate resistance to the
sexual drive shaped in part by external forces of control.

7. The brain stem, or "reptile brain," (MacLean 1975) is a section of the
human brain we share with all vertebrates that controls our defense
system, including all intense feelings. As highly intelligent and vulnerable creatures, we record a wide variety of "dangers" from life.
Some of these, like a mother's excessive stress over a prolonged period, are very real, while events like parents' arguing may be interpreted as extremely dangerous when they are not. Since there is no
way to tell how a particular child will interpret the events of his or
her life, we may well grow up with intense feelings of danger over
real or interpreted incidents that are long forgotten. In adulthood
when we are hearing from our reptile brain, we see situations as
life or death issues, and our choices split into rigid right and wrong
stances. Ambiguity becomes intolerable.

Chapter 2

1. I owe this understanding of the relationship between law and
trust to Foster Cline, M.D., from the Attachment Center, PO Box

2380, Evergreen, Colo. 80439. Dr. Cline trains foster parents to work with severely abused children.

2. As indicated in chapter 1, note 2, Bruce J. Malina (1981, 32–33) addresses the honor- and shame-based cultural context.

3. The wisdom teacher—unlike prophets and scholars of the law who speak in the name of God when they say "Thus says the Lord . . . "—teaches from human experience. Biblical wisdom literature includes Job, Proverbs, Ecclesiastes, and some psalms. Harvey suggests that Jesus' ethical teachings come out of this tradition and are not intended as law that could be used in court.

4. Michael Orlans 1988. Attachment Center.

Chapter 3

1. Joseph Campbell has popularized his finding that every culture has its own stories and traditions of the hero. Popular culture has generalized this idea: we each have an inherent hero journey. We need only discover it. I have found that this rather romantic idea seldom works out for its adherents. People caught up in their search for a hero journey do not seem to be able to accept the routine hardships of life.

2. Jeremias interprets "sinner" to mean that this woman is "either a prostitute or the wife of a man engaged in a dishonorable occupation" (1972, 126).

3. This story has sparked some controversy. Sharon H. Ringe writes:

> The woman's effusive behavior, compounded by the disgrace of her unbound hair, is presented by Luke without explanation. That lack of comment has prompted extensive debate about how Luke intended readers to understand her motivation. The interpretation of her actions is linked, in turn, with the problem of understanding the relationship between love and forgiveness in the final form of the story. Ought one to conclude that her actions are motivated by contrition and thus are the basis on which her sins are declared forgiven? Or ought one to conclude that the incident and parable make the same point, namely, that her actions are the loving acts evoked and made possible by her knowledge of having already been forgiven (1985, 69)?

4. D. W. Winnicott posits that therapists create a "holding environment." In fact, no touch occurs between therapist and client, but rather the therapeutic relationship becomes a safe environment similar to that of a mother holding an infant. Within that environment the "clinical infant" is free to explore psychological distress (1972).

5. Margaret S. Mahler and her colleagues Fred Pine and Anni Bergman (1975) made a major contribution to this discussion.

6. Daniel N. Stern (1985, 19–21) has challenged Mahler's assumption that neonates are autistic.

7. I am using theories and work by Margaret Mahler and by Jerome Kagan. But it is important to note that while psychologists agree that a significant change happens between eighteen months and three years, they disagree about the nature of that change. Popular culture, particularly from the human potential movement of the 1970s, confuses the situation further by identifying narcissism with confidence and idealizing the narcissistic infant: "We are born princes and princesses until our parents and society turn us into frogs." Daniel Stern, whose impressive volume, *The Interpersonal World of the Infant,* compiles laboratory studies with infants and their mothers, proposes that the two-year-old child's growing awareness of language as limiting creative expression of experience occasions distress.

   Clinical implications of these theories are clear: the therapist must furnish a respectful and nurturing environment, as Winnicott has proposed, for individuals to work through wounds originating in childhood. But the implications are terrible for parents. Essentially children become sentimentalized, and parents are the source of all evil.

   Daniel Stern actually proposed that "the terrible twos" are an American issue not occurring in other cultures (Stern's remark was made at a workshop entitled "The Interpersonal World of the Infant: Research and Its Implications for Clinical Theory and Practice," given at Mills College, Oakland, Calif., 22 April 1989). But international studies by developmental psychologist Jerome Kagan demonstrate that, as we noted in chapter 1, two-year-old angst is universal:

   > Two-year-olds become very upset if they are unable to meet a standard for mastery imposed by another person. When a woman approaches a child, picks up some toys,

acts out some brief sequences that are difficult to remember or to implement, and then returns to her chair, children from diverse cultural settings will immediately cry and protest. . . . It is unlikely that these children had been punished for failing to imitate either their parent or another adult. Therefore, we can eliminate a conditioned or acquired fear of punishment as the basis for the distress. I believe that the child invents an obligation to duplicate the adult's action and, additionally, knows that she is unable to do so (1984, 127).

While we must certainly recognize a family's strong influence upon its children, we do not have reliable control over the child's genetic characteristics nor her binding interpretation of family and cultural influences.

Chapter 4

1. Maslow lists the following thirteen characteristics of self-actualized human beings: (1) superior perception of reality; (2) increased acceptance of self, of others, and of nature; (3) increased spontaneity; (4) increase in problem-centering; (5) increased detachment and desire for privacy; (6) increased autonomy and resistance to enculturation; (7) greater freshness of appreciation, and richness of emotional reaction; (8) higher frequency of peak experiences; (9) increased identification with the human species; (10) changed (the clinician would say, improved) interpersonal relations; (11) more democratic character structure; (12) greatly increased creativeness; (13) certain changes in the value system.

2. It is interesting to note, however, that individuals in Maslow's own study did not represent the theory he postulated. Eleanor Roosevelt, for example, was born to a social beauty who complained in her presence to guests about her "ugly duckling daughter." Her father, whom she adored, was an alcoholic. Her mother died when she was eight, and her father when she was nine. As if this were not torment enough, she suffered for years from the infidelity of her famous husband, and yet she, of all United States first ladies, is honored for her rich charity and practical altruism, "the first lady of them all." Without the abandoned concept, "coming to terms" with her environment, this woman's creative contribution is inexplicable. See Wood 1989.

3. Herman Waetjen (1989) translates Jesus' identifying title in this way.

4. I have taken this phrase from H. Richard Niebuhr. Of radical monotheism, he writes:

> When the principle of being is God—i.e., the object of trust and loyalty—then he alone is holy and ultimate sacredness must be denied to any special being. No special places, times, persons or communities are more representative of the One than any others are. . . . A Puritan iconoclasm has ever accompanied the rise of radical faith.
>
> The counterpart of this secularization, however, is the sanctification of all things. Now every day is the day that the Lord has made; every nation is a holy people called by him into existence in its place and time and to his glory; every person is sacred, made in his image and likeness; every living thing, on earth, in the heavens, and in the waters is his creation and points in its existence toward him; the whole earth is filled with his glory; the infinity of space is his temple where all creation is summoned to silence before him. Here is the basis then not only of a transformed ethics, founded on the recognition that whatever is, is good, but of transformed piety or religion, founded on the realization that every being is holy (1943, 52).

5. I owe this excellent phrase to Graham O. Hutchins, a pastor who took "Resurrection Psychology" at Pacific School of Religion in June 1989.

Chapter 5

1. From Montclair Presbyterian Church, Oakland, Calif., June 17, 1990. A version of this saying was on a poster that hung for several years in a multipurpose room.

2. Herman Waetjen consistently uses this title for Jesus, replacing and retranslating the designation, "Son of Man" (1989, 23–26, 70–73).

3. Joseph Weiss and Harold Sampson, together with a team of clinicians at Mount Zion Hospital, San Francisco, have established a theory of development and treatment based on biological altruism or empathy. This theory, called Control Mastery, stresses a client's developing ability to master debilitating feelings. The group has developed a tender and respectful method of treatment. Its one danger lies in a tendency to sentimentalize children. Biological altruism of small children can become idealized as in-

nocent, whole-hearted love. The truth is more along the lines that a child tries in many ways to stabilize his or her home. One woman from a very distressed family explained her experience, "It wasn't so much altruism on my part. Rather I needed a stable home, and since my parents couldn't provide it, I needed to do something to stablize *them*."

4. Father Joseph Chinnici, Professor Brian Hall, Sister Barbara Hazzard, Reverend Marvin Hiles, Father Frank Houdek, Dr. Pat O'Toole, and Reverend Flora Wuellner participated in my project.

5. Many of the following ideas come from the spiritual directors and appear in the chart as well.

6. It is important to note here that for some believers faith develops slowly from childhood and they do not necessarily show all these characteristics.

7. My use of the term *self* roughly corresponds with Heinz Kohut's Self-Psychology.

8. Flora Wuellner, private interview by the author, winter 1984, in Berkeley, Calif.

9. The third, advanced stage of Christian development (see chart 3) is not as significant for discerning genuine helpfulness as distinct from addictive helpfulness, although it may describe some of the experience we observe in Jesus. Religious professionals who direct people through these stages of development assured me that practically no one achieves the furthest heights. The self, so rigid and brittle at the beginning stage of Christian development and in need of more flexibility and firm grounding before an intermediate stage can begin, is observed in full swing. Individuals have personal integrity and spontaneity, a sense of humor, mellowness, and peacefulness. They have a confidence in God's love and guidance without needing to deny their own identity as sinners with failings and inherent longings to be in control. Fluctuations in one's prayer life are accepted with equanimity. A deeper unity with God ensues as well as a heightened dependence. This is not infant symbiosis; rather the growing Christian is very much an individual. Compassion is more reliably God directed. As an individual moves through this advanced stage, personal fulfillment becomes identified with self-donation. Suffering becomes a choice which ensues from ethical decision and action. At the most extreme level of maturity, the cross is willingly embraced,

and we see an abiding peace in the midst of turmoil which we recognize in Jesus on the cross.

Chart 3

Advanced Stage

I. Sense of humor, mellowness, peacefulness. (Hazzard, Wuellner)
Personal integrity, spontaneity. (Houdek)
Acceptance of self as sinner. (J. Chinnici, Houdek)
Full recognition of God's embracing love in spite of our failings. (Wuellner)
Confidence of Spirit moving within one's life. (J. Chinnici)

II. Unity with God, awakening directed by God. (Hiles)
Knowledge through love of God, life directed by God. (O'Toole)
More passive dependence on God. (Hazzard)

III. More compassion, active concern for people. (Hazzard, Wuellner)
Global awareness, concern for right use of power. (Hall)
Simplified values: justice, faithfulness to relationship. Ten Commandments transcended. (Houdek)

IV. Identification with suffering of Christ, concern for suffering and oppressed people. (J. Chinnici)
Personal fulfillment is self-donation. (Houdek)
Suffering isn't done to you; it is the result of what you do. (Hall)

V. God commands and controls life; individual has "mind of Jesus." (Houdek)
Complete union with God, cross willlingly embraced.
Abiding peace in the midst of turmoil. (O'Toole)

Chapter 6

1. Maslow's hierarchy of needs is presented in detail in chapter 3.

2. For example, see John Dominic Crossan 1975 and Kenneth Bailey 1980.

3. See Malina's summary of the concept of limited good, pp. 75–76.

4. For most of this parable I rely on Bailey's excellent rendering of it.

5. The potential offensiveness of each of these stories is consistent with Jesus' intent in the parable of The Good Samaritan.

Chapter 7

1. *Holocaust,* as it is used here, refers to the Nazi treatment of the Jews in the 1930s and 1940s.

Chapter 9

1. His parable of The Wheat and the Weeds (Mt 13:24–30) attests to this, as the Master in the parable instructs his servants to leave the weeds growing in the wheat, lest the wheat be uprooted in an effort to get rid of the weeds.

2. A description by Otto Kernberg of the borderline character disorder, also called personality disorder, appeared in chapter 4 of this book.

3. "Self-Psychology," founded by Heinz Kohut, is a school of thought and practice that has evolved from Freudian psychoanalytic theory. Adherents understand psychological health as having a consistent sense of self apart from others. Some psychodynamic theories suggest that true maturity yields an independence that does not need to rely on others. Self-psychologists differ here; they posit that normal, healthy adults always need "self-objects"; that is, other people who respond to them in ways appropriate to what they initiate. This response may include understanding an idea, applauding and approving, or simply listening attentively. The Self-Psychology method of treatment, which emphasizes consistent empathy, has been very successful in treating character-disordered, also called personality-disordered, people who are extremely fragile and sensitive to criticism.

Chapter 10

1. I owe this image to Cheryl Garlick, a student at New College for Advanced Christian Studies, Berkeley.

2. Beverly Meadows Lieberman, a student at New College Berkeley, observed that Job's friends were distressed by his suffering because it reminded them of their own human vulnerability.

3. Leslie C. Weatherhead asserts that Christians sometimes attribute to God actions for which human beings would be jailed (1978, 11).

Bibliography

Ainsworth, Mary D. Salter, Mary C. Blehar, Everett Waters, and Sally Wall. 1978. *Patterns of Attachment: A Psychological Study of the Strange Situation*. New Jersey: Lawrence Erlbaum Associates.

Alliluyeva, Svetlana. 1967. *Twenty Letters to a Friend*. New York: Harper and Row.

Alter, Margaret G. 1986. "A Phenomenology of Christian Religious Maturity." *Pastoral Psychology* 34, no. 3 (Spring): 151–60.

———. 1989. "An Empirical Study of Christian Religious Maturity: Its Implications for Parish Ministry." *Pastoral Psychology* 37, no. 3 (Spring): 153–60.

Bailey, Kenneth. 1980. *Through Peasant Eyes: More Lucan Parables*. Grand Rapids, Mich.: Wm. B. Eerdmans.

Baker, Howard S., and Margaret N. Baker. 1987. "Heinz Kohut's Self Psychology: An Overview." *The American Journal of Psychiatry* 144, no. 1 (January): 2.

Becker, Ernest. 1973. *The Denial of Death*. New York: The Free Press.

———. 1975. *Escape from Evil*. New York: The Free Press.

Beit-Hallahmi, Benjamin. 1977. "Psychology of Religion 1888–1930: The Rise and Fall of a Psychological Movement." In *Current Perspectives in the Psychology of Religion,* edited by H. Newton Malony. Grand Rapids, Mich.: Wm. B. Eerdmans.

Bellah, Robert N., Richard Madsen, William M. Sullivan, Ann Swidler, and Steven M. Tipton. 1985. *Habits of the Heart*. Berkeley: University of California Press.

Borg, Marcus J. 1987. *Jesus: A New Vision*. San Francisco: Harper and Row.

Bourdieu, Pierre. 1991. *Language and Symbolic Power*. Edited and introduced by John B. Thompson. Cambridge, Mass.: Harvard University Press.

Bowlby, John. 1988. *A Secure Base: Parent-Child Attachment and Healthy Human Development*. New York: Basic Books.

Broucek, Francis J. 1982. "Shame and Its Relationship to Early Narcissistic Developments." *International Journal of Psycho-Analysis* 63:370.

Brueggemann, Walter. 1978. *The Prophetic Imagination*. Philadelphia: Fortress Press.

Buechner, Frederick. 1969. *The Hungering Dark*. San Francisco: Harper and Row.

————. 1973. *Wishful Thinking: A Theological ABC*. New York: Harper and Row.

Coles, Robert. 1967. *A Study of Courage and Fear*. Vol. 1 of *Children of Crisis*. Boston: Little, Brown, and Co.

————. 1977. *Privileged Ones: The Well-off and the Rich in America*. Vol. 5 of *Children of Crisis*. Boston: Little, Brown, and Co.

Cox, Harvey. 1977. *Turning East*. New York: Simon and Schuster.

Crossan, John Dominic. 1975. *The Dark Interval*. Allen, Tex.: Argus Communications.

Cushman, Phillip. 1990. "Why the Self Is Empty: Toward a Historically Situated Psychology." *American Psychologist* 45, no. 5 (May): 600.

Darwin, Charles. 1872. *The Origin of Species*. New York: Doubleday.

Dillard, Annie. 1982. *Teaching a Stone to Talk*. New York: Harper and Row.

Erikson, Erik. H. 1963. *Childhood and Society*. 2nd ed. New York: W. W. Norton and Co.

————. 1969. *Gandhi's Truth*. New York: W. W. Norton and Co.

Feiner, Arthur H., and Edgar A. Levenson. 1968. "The Compassionate Sacrifice: An Explanation of a Metaphor." *Psychoanalytic Review* 55:552–73.

Fortune, Marie M. 1989. *Is Nothing Sacred? When Sex Invades the Pastoral Relationship*. San Francisco: Harper and Row.

Fraiberg, Selma H. 1959. *The Magic Years*. New York: Charles Scribner's Sons.

Freadman, Richard, and Seumas Miller. 1992. *Re-thinking Theory: A Critique of Contemporary Literary Theory and an Alternative Account*. Cambridge: Cambridge University Press.

Freud, Sigmund. 1961. *Civilization and Its Discontents*. New York: W. W. Norton and Co.

Fulghum, Robert. 1988. *It Was on Fire When I Lay Down on It*. New York: Ballantine Books.

Green, Joel B. 1984. *How to Read Prophecy*. Downer's Grove, Ill.: InterVarsity Press.

————. 1992. *The Dictionary of Jesus and the Gospels*. Downer's Grove, Ill.: InterVarsity Press.

————. 1993. "Jesus in the Popular Press: Recent Biographies in Review." *RADIX Magazine* 21, no. 4:24–29.

————. 1994. "Good News to Whom? Jesus and the 'Poor' in the Gospel of Luke." In *Jesus of Nazareth: Lord and Christ: Essays on the Historical Jesus and New Testament Christology,* edited by Joel B. Green and Max Turner. Grand Rapids, Mich.: Wm. B. Eerdmans.

Griffin, Elinor Fitch. 1982. *Island of Childhood: Education in the Special World of Nursery School*. New York: Teachers College Press.

Haley, Jay. 1969. *The Power Tactics of Jesus*. New York: Avon Books.

Hall, Calvin S., and Gardner Lindzey. 1978. *Theories of Personality*. 3rd ed. New York: John Wiley and Sons.

Harvey, A. E. 1990. *Strenuous Commands: The Ethic of Jesus*. Philadelphia: Trinity Press International.

Hoffman, Martin L. 1981. "Is Altruism Part of Human Nature?" *Journal of Personality and Social Psychology* 40, no. 1:121–37.

———. 1982. "Development of Prosocial Motivation: Empathy and Guilt." In *The Development of Prosocial Behavior,* edited by Nancy Eisenberg. New York: Academic Press.

Hughes, Langston. 1971. "Thank You, M'am." In *Tales and Stories for Black Folk,* edited by Toni Bambara. Garden City, N.Y.: Doubleday.

Jeremias, Joachim. 1972. *The Parables of Jesus.* 2nd rev. ed. New York: Charles Scribner's Sons.

Jones, Landon Y. 1980. *Great Expectations: America and the Baby Boom Generation.* New York: Coward, McCann and Geoghegan.

Kagan, Jerome. 1984. *The Nature of the Child.* New York: Basic Books.

Karen, Robert. 1992. "Shame." *Atlantic Monthly* (February): 40.

Kaufman, Gershen. 1985. *Shame: The Power of Caring.* Boston: Schenkman.

Kelsey, Morton. 1978. *Discernment: A Study in Ecstasy and Evil.* New York: Paulist Press.

Kernberg, Otto. 1975. *Borderline Conditions and Pathological Narcissism.* New York: Jason Aronson, Inc.

King, Martin Luther, Jr. 1964. *Why We Can't Wait.* New York: Signet.

Kramer-Rolls, Dana. Forthcoming. "The Transformation of Neurobio-logical Shame and Application to the Ignatian *Spiritual Exercises.*" *Pastoral Psychology.*

Leslie, Robert C. 1965. *Jesus and Logotherapy.* Nashville: Abingdon.

Lewis, C. S. 1960. *The Four Loves.* London: G. Bles.

———. 1964. *Poems.* New York: Harcourt Brace Jovanovich.

MacLean, Paul D. 1975. "On the Evolution of Three Mentalities." *Man-Environment Systems* 5: 213–24.

Mahler, Margaret S., Fred Pine, and Anni Bergman. 1975. *The Psychological Birth of the Human Infant.* New York: Basic Books.

Malina, Bruce J. 1981. *The New Testament World: Insights from Cultural Anthropology.* Atlanta, Ga.: John Knox Press.

Marcus, George E., and Michael M. J. Fischer. 1986. *Anthropology as Cultural Critique: An Experimental Moment in the Human Sciences.* Chicago: University of Chicago Press.

Maslow, Abraham H. 1968. *Toward a Psychology of Being.* 2nd ed. New York: Van Nostrand Reinhold Company.

Menninger, Karl. 1973. *Whatever Became of Sin?* New York: Hawthorne Books.

Metz, Johannes. 1968. *Poverty of Spirit.* New York: Paulist Press.

Miller, Alice. 1981. *The Drama of the Gifted Child.* New York: Basic Books.

Minuchin, Salvador, Braulio Montalvo, Bernard G. Guerney, Jr., Bernice L. Rosman, and Florence Schumer. 1967. *Families of the Slums.* New York: Basic Books.

Mitchell, Raymond N., Jr. 1989. "Behind the Veils: An Integrative Analysis of Shame." Master's thesis, California State University, Hayward.

Morrow, Lance. 1991. "Evil: Does It Exist—or Do Bad Things Just Happen?" *Time,* 10 June, 48–53.

Nathanson, Donald L. 1987. "A Timetable for Shame." In *The Many Faces of Shame,* edited by Donald L. Nathanson. New York: Guilford Press.

Niebuhr, H. Richard. 1943. *Radical Monotheism and Western Culture.* New York: Harper and Row.

———. 1962. *The Responsible Self.* San Francisco: Harper and Row.

Orlans, Michael. 1988. "Treatment of the Unattached: A Model for Therapists." *Attachments* (May). Newsletter.

Ornstein, Anna. 1985. "Survival and Recovery." *Psychoanalytic Inquiry* 5:107, 109–10, 112, 124–25.

Peck, M. Scott. 1983. *People of the Lie: The Hope for Healing Human Evil.* New York: Simon and Schuster.

Perls, Frederick S. 1969. *Gestalt Therapy Verbatim.* Lafayette, Calif.: Real People Press.

Reber, Arthur S. 1985. *The Dictionary of Psychology.* London: Penguin.

Ringe, Sharon. 1985. *Jesus, Liberation, and the Biblical Jubilee.* Philadelphia: Fortress Press.

Rogers, Carl. 1951. *Client-Centered Therapy: Its Current Practice, Implications and Theory.* Boston: Houghton Mifflin.

Sanford, John A. 1984. *Evil: The Shadow Side of Reality.* New York: Crossroads.

Satir, Virginia. 1988. *The New Peoplemaking.* Mountain View: Science and Behavior Books.

Shawn, Wallace, and Andre Gregory. 1981. *My Dinner with Andre.* New York: Grove Press.

Solzhenitsyn, Aleksandr I. 1974. *The Gulag Archipelago: 1918–1965. An Experiment in Literary Investigation.* London: Book Club Associates.

Spitz, Rene. 1965. *The First Year of Life.* Madison, Colo.: International Universities Press.

Spock, Benjamin. 1945. *Baby and Child Care.* New York: Pocket Books.

Stern, Daniel N. 1985. *The Interpersonal World of the Infant: A View from Psychoanalysis and Developmental Psychology.* New York: Basic Books.

Sullivan, Harry Stack. 1953. *The Interpersonal Theory of Psychiatry.* New York: W. W. Norton and Co.

Tillich, Paul. 1948. "You Are Accepted." In *The Shaking of the Foundations.* New York: Charles Scribner's Sons.

———. 1967. *Systematic Theology.* Vol. 1. New York: Harper and Row.

Tomkins, Silvan S. 1963. *Affect/Imagery/Consciousness: II. The Negative Affects.* New York: Springer.

———. 1987. "Shame." In *The Many Faces of Shame,* edited by Donald L. Nathanson. New York: Guilford Press.

Tugwell, Simon. 1980. *The Beatitudes: Soundings in Christian Traditions.* Springfield, Ill.: Templegate.

Van Leeuwen, Mary Stewart. 1985. *The Person in Psychology: A Contemporary Christian Appraisal.* In *Studies in a Christian World View 3.* Grand Rapids, Mich.: Wm. B. Eerdmans.

Viorst, Judith. 1986. *Necessary Losses.* New York: Fawcett.

Waetjen, Herman C. 1976. *The Origin and Destiny of Humanness.* San Rafael, Calif.: Crystal Press.

———. 1989. *A Reordering of Power: A Socio-Political Reading of Mark's Gospel.* Minneapolis: Fortress Press.

Weatherhead, Leslie D. 1978. *The Will of God.* 4th Festival printing. Nashville: Abingdon.

Weiss, Joseph. 1986. "Unconscious Guilt." In *The Psychoanalytic Process: Theory, Clinical Observation, and Empirical Research,* edited by Joseph Weiss, Harold Sampson, and The Mount Zion Research Group. New York: Guilford Press.

Werner, Emily, J. Bierman, and T. French. 1971. *The Children of Kauai: A Longitudinal Study from the Prenatal Period to Age Ten.* Honolulu: University of Hawaii Press.

Williams, H. A. 1979. *The Joy of God: Variations on a Theme.* Springfield, Ill.: Templegate Publishers.

Wink, Walter. 1994. *Holy Week: Interpreting the Lessons of the Church Year, Proclamation 5, Year B.* Minneapolis: Fortress Press.

Winnicott, D. W. 1972. *Holding and Interpretation: Fragment of an Analysis.* New York: Grove Press.

Wood, Jim. 1989. "The First Lady of Them All." *Image Magazine, San Francisco Chronicle,* 25 June.

Index

Ability to respond as responsibility of
receiver, 78–79, 84
Adam and Eve, desire for control
illustrated by, 13, 16
Adolescent period for Americans, 150
Agonistic culture, Middle East as, 171
Al-Anon program for families of alco-
holics, 74–76
Alcoholics Anonymous
forgiveness in, 7
responsibility in, 74
Antitheses in Sermon on the Mount, 25
Archetypes, 58–59, 129
Atonement, 164
Attachment therapists, 29

Baby boomers, 55–56
Bailey, Kenneth, 96–97, 179
Baptism of repentance and death, 67
Bartimaeus, healing of, 72
Beatitudes, paradoxes of, 109–10
Becker, Ernest, 46–47, 60, 110, 143, 148
Bergman, Anni, 40, 174
Berne, Eric, 127
Bonding of mother and infant, 11, 167
Borg, Marcus, xx, 23–24, 39, 89, 94
Bourdieu, Pierre, 171
Bradshaw, John, 58
Brief Symptom Inventory (BSI), 112
Broucek, Francis, 12
Buechner, Frederick, 62, 70, 130–33,
135, 149, 169
Brueggemann, Walter, 122, 130, 133, 136

Campbell, Joseph, 59–60, 173
Certainty
blind system of, 89
danger of, 89–103

as destructive of community, compassion, and blessing, 100
Jesus' disruption of, 92
Children
abused and neglected, 28–29
American enthusiasm for, 55
baby boomer, 55
development of shame in, 11–12,
14–15
as entirely good, 150
idealizing or sentimentalizing, 137,
174
misbehavior to gain attention by, 76
necessity of limits for, 28–29
of privilege, protected, 157, 165
resilient, 172
self-image of, 156
sensitivity to distress in others of,
76
spoiled, 30
vulnerability recognized by, 157
Chinnici, Joseph, 177
Christian development, three-stage
model of, 80–87
advanced stage of, 177–79
beginning level of, 80–81, 86
intermediate level of, 81–87
Christian Experience Inventory (CEI),
112
Civil Rights movement, 78
Client-centered therapy, 54
Cline, Foster, 29–30, 173
Co-dependency, 101
Co-dependent helper, 74
Cognitive shock as cause of shame, 13,
20
Coles, Robert, 157, 165
Collective unconscious, 58, 141–42